Jill and Leon Uris

IRELAND
A Terrible Beauty

The Story of Ireland Today
With 388 Photographs,
Including 108 in Full Color

Now and in time to be,
Wherever green is worn,
Are changed, changed utterly:
A terrible beauty is born.

William Butler Yeats
"Easter 1916"

CORGI BOOKS

We Dedicate This Book
to
OSCAR DYSTEL
KEN McCORMICK
and
JOHN SARGENT

IRELAND A TERRIBLE BEAUTY
A CORGI BOOK 0 552 98013 7

Originally published in Great Britain by
André Deutsch Limited.

PRINTING HISTORY
André Deutsch edition published 1976
Corgi edition published 1977
Corgi edition reprinted 1978
Corgi edition reprinted 1979
Corgi edition reprinted 1981
Corgi edition reprinted 1984
Corgi edition reprinted 1989

Corgi Books are published by Transworld Publishers Ltd.,
Century House, 61-63 Uxbridge Road,
Ealing, London, W 5 5SA
Made and printed in Italy by A. Mondadori Editore, Verona.

Four lines from the poem "Easter 1916" and four lines from "Fergus and the Druid"
from *The Collected Poems of W. B. Yeats.* Reprinted by permission of M. B. Yeats,
Miss Anne Yeats, and Macmillan & Co. of London and Basingstoke and the Macmillan
Co. of Canada.

Poetry from the book *Some Way for Reason* by Maurice James Craig, published by
William Heinemann Ltd. Reprinted by permission of David Higham Associates, Ltd.

Quotation from *The Islandman* by Tomas O Crohan, 1951, translated by Robin Flower.
Reprinted by permission of The Clarendon Press, Oxford.

CONTENTS

Traditionally, until 1922, Ulster included the counties of Donegal, Monaghan, and Cavan, which are now in the Republic.
Northern Ireland, commonly referred to today as Ulster, is a province of Great Britain.

NORTH CHANNEL

DONEGAL
LONDONDERRY (DERRY)
ANTRIM
Northern Ireland
U L S T E R
TYRONE
DOWN
FERMANAGH
ARMAGH
MONAGHAN
CAVAN
LOUTH

SLIGO
LEITRIM

MAYO

ROSCOMMON
LONGFORD
MEATH

ATLANTIC OCEAN

CONNAUGHT
WEST MEATH
DUBLIN
IRISH SEA

GALWAY
OFFALY
KILDARE

LEINSTER
LEIX
WICKLOW

CLARE

Republic of Ireland
CARLOW

LIMERICK
TIPPERARY
KILKENNY

WEXFORD

MUNSTER
WATERFORD

KERRY

CORK

ST. GEORGE'S CHANNEL

N

0   MILES   50

PREFACE

THAT SOFT IRISH WEATHER

There are an estimated quarter of a million archaeological sites and antiquities, registered and unregistered, within Ireland. Likewise, the number of castles, fairs, horse and flower shows, quaint pubs, picturesque cottages, islands and islanders, stone walls, holy wells and beds of saints, donkey carts, and peat bogs runs into staggering figures. By no manner of means do we attempt to present an all-inclusive portrait.

We were lured there by an intriguing people, their sometimes magnificent, sometimes harsh land, and, mostly, their poignant history. Our aim was to find the keys to that story which would clarify so much of the mystery and puzzlement of recent events and simultaneously photograph everyone and everything wherever the search took us.

The way was ten thousand miles long, which is a sizable distance when you consider that Ireland is less than a third the size of our home state of Colorado. We traveled by a number of conveyances, mostly automobile, on some decent and some indecent roads. We called it a day in two dozen different hostelries, talked to as many Irishmen as there are registered castles, bit off the better part of a year, and even learned to live with the perennially prevailing mists, affectionately called "that soft Irish weather."

Indeed, many special trips not vital to the actual story were laid on chasing after scenery or the haunted remoteness of the islands as well as the necessary ventures into the staccato of gunfire. We calculated that both were needed to gain the necessary insight to define a true cross section and to comprehend what this place and these people were all about.

Some of the Hayes clan of County Wexford or a Hanley from Roscommon might feel slighted herein, but Ireland is too vast and complex in its story for two people to cover it comprehensively in less than a decade. We made no pretense at attempting to.

What we do have here is a social, historical, and political commentary on what we consider to be the guts of the matter of a unique people and their lovely but sorrowed island. This is our point of view on the "troubles" that have plagued Ireland for the fatter part of a millennium.

You might call it a love song. For those among them who have it to give, and they are the vast majority, nowhere are friendship and kindness lavished more freely on the stranger. The thought of these people will warm us for all our years. Even the memory of "that soft Irish weather."

Jill and Leon Uris

7

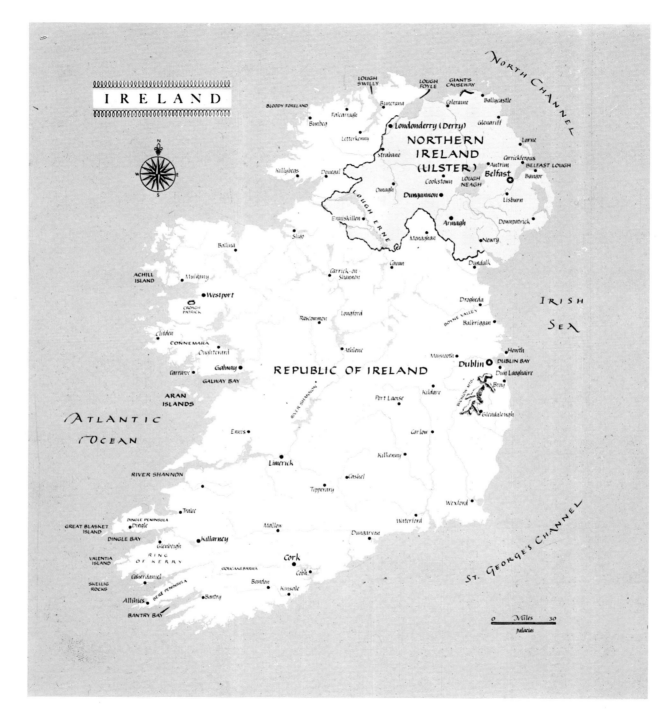

Book One

THE REPUBLIC

1. AN UNCONQUERABLE SPIRIT ENDURES THROUGH A TRAGIC HISTORY

Two facts predominate in the molding of the Irish character and the shape of her story. First, Ireland is an island. Secondly, she remained Catholic during the Reformation.

Small subject peoples such as the ancient Hebrews, the Afghans, and the Poles had the geographic misfortune to be land bridges crossed indiscriminately by conquering armies whose hordes flowed west to east and east to west, pillaging, plowing under, dispersing, and homogenizing.

In the beginning there was only the uninhabited land of Ireland after the recession of the Ice Age. From the Stone Age on down through the British, this isolated island had to be sought out deliberately.

Major incursions were relatively few, but each left its own indelible mark. Stone Age aborigines were displaced by the Celts at the dawn of the Christian Era. A highly advanced pagan people collected from a variety of Central European and sub-Asian tribes their laws and organization; above all, their language and mysticism earmark and flavor the Irish people.

Around the eighth century, after the Celts, Danish rovers established coastal cities and routes to the world beyond, infusing their own physical features on the Celts, best portrayed by vivid red hair.

In the twelfth century Nicholas Breakspeare became the only English Pope, Hadrian IV, and as such granted Henry II of Britain a papal bull allowing him to take the land of Ireland as his "inheritance," establishing the quasi-legal basis for conquest and occupation.

At the King's behest, Strongbow the Norman invaded, subdued the Celtic clans, and claimed Ireland for the Crown.

The Danes were ultimately driven from the country, and the Normans integrated so totally that they became more Irish than the Irish.

What was to form the oil and water that would never mix was that final massive intrusion by the British at the outset of the seventeenth century. It is difficult to pinpoint the exact time when the "troubles" began, but for certain it had something to do with the alien British on their soil—be it eight hundred years of occupation or four hundred years of intense colonization. Ireland has been cruelly and stupidly administered and her people shamefully persecuted, with every sort of indignity brought to bear. The most wanton penal laws legislated by a civilized Western nation denied the Irish Catholics every human and material right. In the mid-nineteenth century the great famine was little more than a subtle exercise at "gentleman's genocide." The land has been stripped naked through court intrigues and run red to the sound of clanging armor and bellowing cannon in an epic of boundless greed.

Through it all a magnificent people have survived with their own unique identity intact. They are as warm and lovely as any on this earth. Their wit is incomparable. Their use of words and language has enriched life wherever they have touched it.

The largest and saddest export of this country has always been her people. The stricken land, a ponderous religion, and a tortured foreign occupation have made it impossible for decades of Irish to exist in their own country. And so, much of the Irish glory has been won by a far-flung diaspora, but whether at home or in exile, few people of this size have made such a dynamic impact on the world.

In the European experience, invading armies have overrun that continent from Mongolia, Islam, and the barbaric reaches, and they have overrun each other. Each chapter of conquest has left an infusion of its culture and lore long after its tide receded. Eventually these customs found their way to Ireland, which is, after all, the last outpost of Europe. It has become a depository for the folkways of a dozen cultures, the haven of the last great peasantry of the West. All this, mixed in with their own Celtic bizarreness and the deeply practiced mystical aspects of Catholicism, have given them the universal image of leprechaun people.

Here is a last look at a place and a people who will soon lose much of the magic that sets them apart. They embark, somewhat reluctantly, on a confusing journey into the twentieth century with the smoke of battle still raging and stinging the nostrils. It is a battle for freedom joined many hundred years before. The full cycle of imperialism is coming to a close after four hundred years in the same place it started. Ireland, England's first colony, is destined to be her last.

BROWNE'S HILL DOLMEN

The first positive evidence of human settlement is to be found in a variety of burial grounds, some dating back to 6000 B.C. in the form of court cairns, passage and gallery graves, and portal dolmens.

In a pasture near Carlow the Browne's Hill dolmen marks the entrance to a Stone Age grave site. It is the largest in Ireland, with its capstone estimated to weigh over a hundred tons.

The considerable feat of raising it was accomplished by building a mound, dragging the capstone up on it, then digging the earth away and carting it off.

A sparseness of timber and topsoil plus the preponderance of rock as a building material have left a myriad of exquisitely preserved stone antiquities. These ring forts on the Kerry peninsula and Inishmaan and dozens like them, along with hill forts, promontory forts, and crannogs built in the middle of artificial lakes, were overrun by the Celts with their superior iron weaponry. Many of the buildings remained in use until the Middle Ages.

Irish history begins with the coming of the Celts, who laid the nation's foundation with the geographic division of the land among the clans and the setting of their pales. Choosing the kings and chieftains of each mini-state was through popular election. A universal social order and system of law prevailed along with a common language. The rich culture emanated from those learned men, the Druid priests.

Patrick, captured in Britain by Irish coastal marauders, served in slavery as a shepherd until his escape to the Continent. After Romanization he returned to Ireland and converted it to Christianity in the fifth century.

(Above) *At Skellig Michael, off the coast of Kerry, this ancient monastery is attributed to St. Finan. It sits on a shelf of a cliff six hundred feet over the ocean and must be reached by a perilous climb of six hundred eroded slab steps cut into the rock. An early Celtic cross marks the last station of a surrogate Via Dolorosa standing beside a dry stone beehive-shaped monk's cell in a nearly perfect state.*

13

(Left) *This superb oratory is perhaps the prime example of the mortarless construction accomplished by a painstaking corbeling of huge flat stones.*

GLENDALOUGH—A Monastic City in the Wicklow Mountains founded by St. Kevin in the Sixth Century

Ireland's freedom from invasion for several centuries enabled her to embark on a golden age during which her scholars and missionaries were the light of the Western world. Monastic cities such as this functioned as both religious baronies and universities.

St. Columba was the giant of his time, no less a figure than St. Patrick himself. He was the first great Irishman of letters, patron of the poets, founder of Derry, and father of Irish missionaries who converted the Picts, Angles, and Saxons of Britain to Christianity.

Another Titan, St. Columbanus, and his monks journeyed into France establishing monasteries and missions. His predecessors ranged over western Europe from the Netherlands and Germany into the Alps and Italy. Many functioned as the learned men in courts clear up to Charlemagne.

(Right) *A Celtic High Cross stands guard before one of the seventy remaining Round Towers built between the ninth and twelfth centuries as belfries. They served as lookout posts, storehouses, and refuge centers from Viking raiders.*

STRONGBOW'S DOWRY—Dunamase Castle

WATERFORD—The Danish Kingdom of CUAN-NA-GROITH

In A.D. 800 Viking longboats scourging the European coasts made their Irish debut with twenty-five years of hit-and-run raids by small freebooter parties. Monasteries, poorly defended and always an excellent source of provisions, were prime targets.

As the raids picked up momentum, operating in large fleets, bases were established for inland marches. Later these became Danish and Norse "kingdoms" and today are the cities of Dublin, Limerick, Cork, and Waterford. The river Shannon became a Viking waterway.

The Viking colonies continued on as powerful independent states, traders to the outside world and artisans.

It was an era of constant warfare between Irish kingdoms. Out of it all emerged Brian Boru, King of Munster, who, in defeating the O'Neills, became sole claimant to the throne of Tara, symbolic of High King of Ireland. Under Brian the country was unified as never before, but even so, the game of kings went on.

In a grandiose power play the Norsemen and Danes allied with the King of Leinster and gathered in Viking soldiers from their colonies in Scotland and the Isle of Man. An epic battle took place on Good Friday in the year of 1014 at Clontarf on Dublin Bay.

Brian Boru, too ancient to join the fight, awaited news in his tent. As the Vikings and their allies plunged into retreat, one of the foe, Brodar, wandered into Brian's tent and killed him.

Ireland's grief was overwhelming as Brian Boru was put to rest in Armagh, the diocese of St. Patrick.

The Vikings had come within a whisper of becoming the dominant force in Ireland. After the Battle of Clontarf, their time was at its end.

Laudabiter, the papal bull defining the granting of Ireland to Henry II of England, found a willing champion. The original Norman invaders of England had been given free settlement of Wales and were spoiling for Ireland. Their opportunity came when Dermot, the deposed King of Leinster, turned to Henry for help. He, in turn, granted permission for an army to be raised from the Welsh Normans.

Richard Fitzgilbert de Clare, Earl of Pembroke, landed in Waterford in 1170. The Irish kings, who had long engaged in unsophisticated tribal warfare, were no match for the modern arms and tactics of the conquest-bent Normans and capitulated in short order. Pembroke was respectfully renamed Strongbow.

Henry became wary of Strongbow's intentions, followed him to Ireland with a massive force, and quickly obtained pledges of allegiance from the chieftains and from the Church. He then established a government in the annexed Norse kingdom of Dublin.

Strongbow took Eva, a legendary beauty and daughter of Dermot, as his wife. As part of the dowry he was gifted with Dunamase Castle, a vital strongpoint which had seen bloody battle from ancient days through the Cromwellian War.

For the Normans it was a new motherland and they peopled it with the likes of such great families as Burke, Fitzgerald, Joyce, Dalton, Roche, and Barry.

England embarked heavily on the business of consolidating its position through the medium of a subverted Irish Parliament.

Over a period of generations, intermarriage with the Irish and mutual hatred for the English converted the Normans to total Irishness.

The Norman experience climaxed during the Reformation as Ireland remained steadfastly Catholic. When Henry VIII declared himself King of Ireland and Protestant head of the Irish Church, he triggered a series of rebellions by Norman and Celtic septs alike.

England's retaliation was swift and total.

THE VANQUISHING OF THE CLANS AND THE FLIGHT OF THE EARLS
—Dunboy Castle

The Fitzgeralds and Shane O'Neill and Black Hugh O'Donnell and Fitzmaurice of Munster all had their go at it in sixty-five years of uprisings.

A last hurrah was to come as ultimate battle lines were drawn with the British fleet and forces under Lord Mountjoy landing at Kinsale in 1602.

Red Hugh O'Donnell surrendered after a foolhardy attack, as did the Spanish allies under Del Aguila. The clans were issued a crushing defeat with Hugh O'Neill, the Earl of Tyrone, fleeing back to their ancient lair in Ulster.

The O'Sullivans reeled back to their own stronghold in Dunboy Castle on the Bere peninsula. Here, legend and fact intermingle inseparably. The British inflicted a massacre. Some say they refused to allow the O'Sullivans to surrender, and some say the O'Sullivans took their lives by their own hands with defeat imminent. A few escaped and embarked on an epic march to County Leitrim.

This epilogue to the Battle of Kinsale marked the end of Norman and Celtic Ireland.

This abandoned mansion eerily guards the site of Dunboy Castle.

DUBLIN CASTLE
—Government Without Consensus

Down through the centuries Dublin Castle held the administrative offices and served as residence for the Crown's highest representatives. The very words "Dublin Castle" became synonymous with intrigue and tyranny. From here was crafted a social order that permitted the vassal state to be exploited with the least resistance. A series of alliances were effected against the Irish masses that assured the principle of "divide and rule."

The cornerstone of British power lay with the Ascendancy, in the persons of Anglo-Protestants who crossed the water to get their piece of Ireland as reward for service or for imperial adventure. The Ascendancy not only accounted for the landed gentry but formed Ireland's core of professionals—doctors, lawyers, teachers—bankers, factory owners, and upper-rank merchants. They were a privileged class intent on keeping it that way.

A second force was the loyalty of that solid block of Scots planted in Ulster for the prime purpose of loyalty.

The fledgling Catholic middle class considered the Crown a benefactor and provider. These old-stock Irish were content enough to turn their backs to the raging poverty and injustice so long as "business went on as usual."

Not least stood a Catholic Hierarchy who went along with and assisted efforts to impose English culture at the expense of the Gaelic heritage. With their direct link to the people, the Church rendered even more valuable assistance to the British by purging generation after generation of their flock of nationalistic aspirations.

But the fine hand of Dublin Castle was best to be seen in the using of impoverished Irish against impoverished Irish in the military and police.

The Castle now functions as the state apartments of the Republic for ceremonial purposes, but odors of arrogance and duplicity linger on.

19

Evicted Irish were given a dim choice of exile to the barren, infertile reaches of Connaught beyond the river Shannon or a quick trip to hell at the end of a Puritan sword. It is estimated that over one hundred thousand boys and girls between fourteen and sixteen, orphaned by murder, were shipped as slaves to the British West Indies.

HELL OR CONNAUGHT

—A Land of Desolation

The Irish land grab was consummated with bottomless gluttony, the land sold at bargain prices to worthy English in massive hunks up to baronies in size. To get rid of those pesky O'Neills, the clan was blatantly dispossessed in Ulster and replaced by a hundred and fifty thousand Scottish Lowlanders.

Long-standing grievances plus the creation of a landless class of peasantry erupted into an inevitable uprising. In 1641, Owen Roe O'Neill, nephew of Red Hugh, returned from Europe to lead a civil war that was to last for eleven years and reduce the population by nearly half.

In Ulster, thousands of Scottish colonizers were murdered in the wake of Catholic wrath. This day of vengeance was to create an eternal pall of fear over Protestant heads and cement that siege mentality which plagued them from the day they came to Ulster to serve as a crown outpost.

Bloodletting reached epic proportions as Oliver Cromwell, fresh from his own political strife, landed in Ireland. In crushing the rebellion he inflicted the most notable massacres in Irish history. Entering battle on a hymn and a prayer, he sought God's blessings and gave thanks for each day of slaughter.

There has been an effort by some to equate the atrocities committed by both sides, but Cromwell made the Irish look piddling by the sheer number of murders. It is also apparent that a man who kills to regain his stolen land must be more just than a man who kills to retain the land he has stolen and does so in the name of God.

The savagery of Cromwell's army was rewarded by the seizure of two and a half million acres of the best remaining Irish land and the parceling of it out as back pay and as financing for his various campaigns.

Cromwell's outrage was followed several decades later by further outrage in the enactment of the Penal Laws which denied Catholics every human right. They were forbidden to own land, receive education, vote, hold public office, practice law or their religion, or receive justice—or at best were severely restricted in pursuit of these rights. A final insult was in the form of a tithe to the Anglican Church. One English Lord Chancellor opined that he could not assume there was, under law, any such person as an Irish Catholic.

The Penal Laws were to last for more than a century, with the Irish peasant now reduced to one of the lowest forms of human life on planet earth.

THE ASCENDANCY

Today, the Republic of Ireland is ninety-five per cent Catholic, but the Anglo-Ascendancy continues to hold a position of wealth and power many times more important than its numbers.

Some of the Ascendancy exist in English enclaves or hole up in dank manor houses that display great oil portraits of Cromwell or King William of Orange, and they ride to the hounds, listen only to the BBC, read the London *Times* on special order, and otherwise still look to England. Permeated with the colonizer's mentality, they exist as strangers in their own country.

There has, however, been a continuing tradition of dynamic Protestants whose positive contribution to Ireland as Ireland has been equally effective. The first stirrings of nationalism were inspired by the French Revolution and established a pattern by which Ireland was to seek self-determination. In a two-pronged assault the Irish Parliament of Henry Grattan sought liberation through parliamentary action, while Theobald Wolfe Tone sought it with the gun. Robert Emmet's speech from the dock sounded the battle cry of Irish Republicanism. Two generations later Charles Stewart Parnell created an effective Irish Party in Westminster. Sir Roger Casement was hanged as a result of his participation in the Easter Uprising of 1916, and Erskine Childers was martyred in the Civil War that followed. On May 30, 1973, the son of Erskine Childers was elected President of Ireland.

Among Ireland's immortal writers of Ascendancy stock were Oliver Goldsmith, Jonathan Swift, George Bernard Shaw, Oscar Wilde, Thomas Moore, and William Butler Yeats.

WESTPORT HOUSE

John Browne was sent to County Mayo in 1585 for the purpose of making the chieftains accept the Crown. Mayo was the ancestral lair of the legendary O'Malley sept, pirates of the first order.

Three generations later his heir, Colonel John Browne, began Westport House on the site of the O'Malley castle-fortress destroyed by Cromwell.

Colonel Browne remained loyal to James II, the dispossessed English Catholic King, in his struggle for the crown with William of Orange. He was there at the Siege of Limerick when capitulation all but destroyed the family's fortunes.

Seat of the Marquess of Sligo, Westport House today has been converted into one of the leading historical attractions in the country.

The Earl of Altamont, Jeremy Ulich, son of the tenth marquess, welcomes guests in a more casual way these days.

THE WHITE DEER OF MALLOW

Symbolic of the continued presence of the Ascendancy are the white deer of Mallow. Legend has it that this unusual herd was sired by a pair of white stags presented by Queen Elizabeth I to her goddaughter Elizabeth Jephson at Mallow Castle nearly four hundred years ago.

A NATION OF EXILES

After a time there was an erosion of the Penal Laws, and Catholics were elevated from peonage to second-class citizenship. However, the Irish Parliament under Henry Grattan was too liberal and reform-bent for the British to stomach. On subduing the rebellion of the United Irish in 1798 under Theobald Wolfe Tone, the Crown decided on a new tactic. With General Cornwallis, of American Revolution fame, as the British Viceroy, the Irish were coerced and bribed into dissolving their own Parliament and uniting with England. The scheme repelled even the man who executed the plan. Some Irish went to Westminster in Commons and Lords but were relegated to a powerless and ridiculed minority. It was to be three decades after the Act of Union before the first Catholic, Daniel O'Connell, was able to take a seat in the British Parliament.

None of these maneuvers or new "freedoms" meant much to the Irish peasantry, who continued on the tightrope of survival. Under a law designed to keep Catholics from gaining too much land, farms and family debts had to be divided among all the sons. With the large Irish families, the land was divided and redivided by marriage until the average size fell to less than fifteen acres.

The potato became the staple of the peasant's existence. It was easy to plant and required little attention, and an average-sized family could get by on a few acres of them. Eventually the land became played out, setting the stage for disaster.

From 1845 to 1850 a blight struck the potato crop. Between British ineptness and callous landlordism, a great famine raged out of control.

Absentee landlords, many in heavy personal debt and mortgaged to the hilt from aristocratic overspending, ordered that those unable to meet their rents be evicted. Land agents with military escort razed tens of thousands of cottages to the ground, leaving their occupants homeless. At the same time other crops were seized, and the pens at the shipping ports bulged with cattle for export. There was ample food within Ireland to prevent famine, but the landlords and business community would have no tampering with their profits. While people starved to death, cattle by the thousands were shipped to England.

Relief, such as it was, was too little and too late. An estimated million peasants died of hunger and disease. Another million fled the country in floating coffins, many among them dying at sea. Although these Irish were supposed to be British citizens, the doors of England were shut in their faces, forcing them to America and Canada, where more thousands landed stricken and soon succumbed.

SENDING HOME THE SLATES *A traditional measure of the success of the son or daughter who has made it well in the new country can be seen in a grand slate roof on the cottage or in the size and beauty of the monuments erected for the mothers and fathers left behind.*

Westminster, always quick to legislate its own favorable position in Ireland, did a complete turnaround on the succession of land. After the famine it became illegal to divide land. One son became the inheritor. The rest of the family had to move on to the cities or emigrate. From the famine on, Ireland has been compelled to give away her sons and daughters in tragic emigrations.

The great famine came bitterly close to breaking the Irish

spirit. An entire social pattern changed from early to late marriages, from an effervescent peasantry to a cautious, religiously subjugated people. The close-knit family unit was shattered. The specter of the famine would remain forever.

The British have a magnificent sense of justice second to that of no other people on earth, but they seem to abandon it when it comes to the Irish, whom they largely consider to be a nation of quaint, lying, lazy, ignorant, shiftless drunks. When a great power reduces a defeated people to where they have surrendered even their dignity, nothing decent, holy, or just gives that great power any right to condemn or berate those who have been the victims of their creation.

COBH—HARBOR OF TEARS *This was the last sight of Ireland seen by hundreds of thousands of her sons and daughters forced from their homeland by famine and poverty.*

THE GAP OF MAMORE IN COUNTY DONEGAL *A surrealistic wayside shrine overlooks Lough Swilly.*

2. THE CATHOLIC HIERARCHY
—Questions Replace Blind Obedience

Until recently few authorities were as absolute as an Irish bishop in his diocese and the priest in his parish. In the agrarian society the priest was usually the only literate man and dispensed justice in petty quarrels, advised in business matters, and oversaw health and education, as well as religion. No town would dare open a new pub or hotel without his consent. His wishes were as powerful as the constituted government. Often as not he was considered infallible and a possessor of supernatural powers. Once he was ordained, even his own family held him in awe.

To perpetuate this position, an abundance of priests were produced. Some twenty thousand ordained priests manned the twenty-eight Irish dioceses, as well as English-speaking parishes abroad and the overseas missions. This force was augmented by thirteen thousand nuns and two thousand teachers in the Christian Brothers order.

The horn of plenty stems from the unparalleled devotion of the people, which has made priesthood the highest human calling.

No small amount of this success can be attributed to Irish "momism." Irish sexual appetites are generally low key. The women are notoriously unfulfilled. Such women, who have found little or nothing from sex, see no wrong in urging their sons into a life of celibacy. Priesthood enhances the mothers' own social status. A general custom is to give a son to the Church out of rote. The Irish lad is particularly suited for priesthood by a tradition of celibacy that goes back to monastic days.

The root of the woman's problem can generally be found in the moral dictatorship imposed from childhood which stifles, condemns, and riddles with guilt every natural sexual impulse. The Church has lately realized that it has to modify its suppression of normal human behavior, but this revelation came too late to salvage the wreckage it made in Ireland.

Irish boys grew up doted over by an adoring mom. Playing around with the girls invited the disaster of the "burden" of marriage. It was far easier to have Mom looking after him and to find his companionship with fellow members of the Irish drinking brotherhood. There is a sorry joke about this in Ireland. One asks, "What is the definition of an Irish queer?" The answer, "A man who prefers girls to drink." When marriage does come, it is usually late in life and with finality, for what follows is an annual baby parade.

No Christian people are so dedicated to their faith or have it woven so closely in the very fabric of life. However, under the outward veneer there is a great deal of "automatic Catholicism." They are saturated with it from birth and forced into a close style of communal living with no choice but to conform or be ostracized. Too much of the mass and of prayer is recited without meaning in listless monotone by men driven into the church out of fear of the priests or what the neighbors will think.

Actually, Catholics of Italy, France, and the Latin nations are governed by the same dogma and moral ponderousness. However, in matters of sex the French and Italians and other Latins just didn't take the Church all that seriously.

The Irish did. Perhaps the Irish accepted Church autocracy because they had lived under one kind of autocrat or the other for centuries, and subservience had become a part of life.

During the penal days of the eighteenth century, priests were hidden in caves, and mass and the perpetuation of the religion were done in secret. Because their privations and risks were mutual, a close bond was formed between shepherd and flock.

As the Penal Laws receded, the British were Johnny on the spot in establishing an Irish theological institution along lines they could control. To this end, the beginnings of St. Patrick's College at Maynooth were made in 1795; it was staffed with hard-line Jansenists from France, who turned out a new mold of domineering priests.

With emancipation, the churchmen went on a building binge during the 1800s and cloaked themselves in a kind of luxury that set them apart from the people, thereby breaking the bonds of penal days.

As their power grew, they indulged in a little ecclesiastical bigotry of their own. Catholics at first were forbidden by the Protestants to attend Trinity College in Dublin. The restriction was continued by the Hierarchy itself until very recent years. For centuries Catholic churchmen never set foot in either of the two Protestant cathedrals in Dublin, although the doors had long been open to them. They went so far as to forbid Catholics to attend weddings or funerals of their Protestant neighbors.

On the issue of national liberation the Hierarchy has been consistent in condemnation of the United Irish Uprising of 1798 and its immortal leader Theobald Wolfe Tone, the Fenian Uprising of the mid-1800s, the Land League struggling for equity for the peasant, the Irish Republican Brotherhood, its successor the Irish Republican Army, and the Easter Uprising of 1916.

In 1922 Ireland concluded a Treaty with Britain creating a Free State. This was rejected by a huge faction of the IRA, including their leader, Eamon de Valera, and Civil War followed. The rebels were condemned by being excommunicated. Later, de Valera returned to their good graces.

Perhaps the shabbiest performance of all was the vilification of Charles Stewart Parnell, the Protestant who fought the Catholic battle in Westminster by carving out and leading a unified, effective Irish Party. Parnell, like no other Irish politician before him, earned the respect and fear of the British. After a divorce scandal the bishops went at him like jackals, sending him, disillusioned, to an early grave.

Although the Hierarchy claims the Church isn't in politics, its desires have been legislated as national law in matters of abortion, contraceptives, and divorce. The no-divorce edict, in particular, has caused terrible misery to women and children abandoned by husbands who have fled overseas.

The Church has a virtual strangle hold on the public education system, in which every teacher and curriculum has to be approved.

Much of the welfare and health facility has been in Church hands since the creation of the Free State. It was in a shambles, with TB a particular scourge. During the 1950s a coalition government enacted a "mother and child" scheme to provide desperately needed medical care. In what was to be the most reactionary position of the modern era, the bishops led the assault in destroying the plan under the guise that it would invite socialism.

In all fairness it must be said that on a number of occasions a substantial part of the population chose to ignore the various condemnations, and there have always been a goodly number of priests, utterly devoted to their parishioners, who have likewise chosen to look the other way or downright defy the bishops.

In today's Ireland, waves are being made. Many younger priests are questioning everything including celibacy. Other priests are leaving the Church in such numbers that the once fat ranks are thinning. New recruits are falling behind in number. No longer does the youth seek priesthood, for the pros-

pects it offers simply are not that attractive any more.

In Maynooth a nucleus of liberal and progressive priests and educators are tackling the mounting problems with insight and wisdom but, by and large, they throw the old guard into a fright. The day of a dynamic reform movement is still far off, and it may well come too late.

As for the people, there is a national preoccupation with the once forbidden questions of birth control, abortion, and divorce. Censorship has had much of the starch knocked out of it, although blood and gore are still more acceptable than sex. Recently the Irish people voted to delete the special position of the Catholic Church from their constitution. The ban on contraceptives is now under heavy constitutional scrutiny.

Why, then, in the light of this sketchy showing by the Hierarchy, have the people remained so uncommonly devout? Massive injections of fear and guilt have certainly played a part. Until the great famine and well into this century the Irish were a deprived and largely uneducated people. Life had dealt a crushing set of circumstances. A respite from despair was mandatory. Far too many found it in drink. They needed to adopt a kind of fantasy world to escape the anguish, and the price for entrance into it was blind, unquestioning faith and an acceptance of the power and authority of the Church.

Once this house is entered, it cannot be escaped all that easily. Thinkers have groped with this problem without answer. Those who do rebel are generally filled with venom, tormented by their own stand.

The Church is also blessed with a great number of wise and self-sacrificing humanitarians who did God's image no harm at all, and who carried out necessary work for a people desperately dependent on them. There was no hole too black to keep the needed priest out.

With all the arguments against the educational system, some good must have come across. Today's generation is as bright, sharp, and representative as any and more than likely educated by Christian Brothers and nuns. These teachers work in absolute dedication and poverty.

And how many sick eyes have fluttered open to gaze at the nursing nun whose smile and faith brought instant hope? Where the poor dwelt and orphans sought to grasp a way to life, the nuns were there. Maybe they didn't do the best job in the world, but they kept the Irish together.

Much of the responsibility was palmed off by a government not ready to take on the responsibility themselves. They continued to use the Church as a crutch and let the Church be scapegoat for not doing the job well.

With all said and done, there is but one basic truth: without the Catholic religion and the priesthood, the Irish race would not have survived.

CASHEL

Crowning the plain of Tipperary, St. Patrick's rock marks one of the most important historical sites in Ireland. Legend has it that during Patrick's ten-year stay he first used the shamrock here in demonstrating the Trinity. The traditional home of the Kings of Munster, "the rock" was more than likely fortified in the fourth century, over a hundred years before Patrick's visit. As the political and religious center of the province it has played host to an unbroken string of battles, consecrations, and coronations. After the Norman conquest, Henry II proceeded from his landing in Waterford to Cashel to receive the homage of the Gaelic chieftains and the allegiance of the Bishop of Cashel.

St. Patrick's rock holds a treasury of antiquities dating back to pagan time. The choir of Cormac's Chapel once carried a stone roof crafted by Rhineland masons. This mini-cathedral was built in 1124 and remains as the masterpiece of the ancient churches.

CROAGH PATRICK—The Holy Mountain

Soaring twenty-five hundred feet over Clew Bay in County Mayo, Croagh Patrick plays host to an annual pilgrimage said to have its origin in pagan times with the Druid priests of the Celts.

On the last Sunday of July thousands upon thousands gather to reaffirm their devotion or seek blessings or perhaps even a miracle. Many humiliate themselves by making the all-night climb barefooted over jagged stone. At dawn the summit is reached, that place where Patrick is said to have fasted forty days and nights, afterward casting the snakes out of Ireland.

DERRYNANE ABBEY—Home of the Liberator

The bittersweet story of Daniel O'Connell began in 1775 in Cahirciveen, County Kerry, a few miles from his lifelong home. He was adopted by an uncle named Hunting Cap who had made it huge in smuggling. Denied schooling in Ireland, O'Connell was educated in England and France. As a Catholic lawyer, he was a rarity in Ireland.

The man was utterly dedicated to a two-stage goal: emancipation for Catholics and repeal of the Act of Union with England. To this end he formed a Catholic Association and in a stroke of genius made it a movement of the masses by providing membership at a contribution of a penny a month.

Committed to nonviolence, his monster rallies unified the Catholics for a redress of ancient and endless grievances. The early battles were particularly aimed at the tithe to the Anglican Church and Britain's "right" to veto the selection of Catholic bishops.

O'Connell swept an election in County Clare in 1823 but was denied a seat in Westminster by his refusal to take the parliamentary oath of fidelity to the Protestant faith. He fought on to win his first goal with passage of a Bill for the Emancipation of Non-Anglicans. In 1829 he took his seat, uncontested. In 1841 he was elected the first Catholic mayor of Dublin of the new era.

With momentum in full surge to repeal the Act of Union, a monster rally at Tara, home of the High Kings, drew a crowd of a million people.

All of it was getting a bit much for Dublin Castle. He was put on trial for "defying the laws of Her Britannic Majesty in Ireland," found guilty, and sentenced to prison. The House of Lords hastily reversed the judgment to head off bloodshed, which O'Connell himself detested.

Two more years of turmoil and spotty success ravaged his mind and body. In the early part of 1847 he called it quits, traveling to Italy in an attempt to regain his health. He died in Genoa several months later, realizing Ireland had embarked on the great famine. The body was returned to Ireland, where he was buried in Dublin.

Some historians look upon the O'Connell era as one of mixed blessings. Full emancipation of the Church set it off on a course of autocratic excesses. Far more disastrous was the effect on the Protestant community, which interpreted it as a threat to its existence. Protestant factions unified as never before, now wearing an ugly cloak of sectarianism.

Daniel O'Connell, through peaceful means and brilliance, sounded a call to his people, who had been smeared in the muck for two hundred and fifty years. He gave them dignity and a reasonable chance to go forward to self-determination, that second goal, which eluded him.

It was fitting that he requested that his heart be embalmed upon death and taken to Rome.

ARMAGH—Northern Ireland

Armagh was selected by Patrick as the seat of his church, and the Archbishop of Armagh is likewise the primate of the Roman Catholic Church. Two St. Patrick's Cathedrals rival each other, the twin-spired one on the left belonging to St. Patrick's Catholic heirs while the one on the right is the headquarters of the Anglican Church of Ireland. Patrick's establishment here ended the pagan era and ushered in Christianity. Graffiti on the lower wall are addressed to the British Army, and accompanying bomb damage and sectarian murders in this sacred city give rise to serious consideration of whether the Christian message ever got through.

MAYNOOTH, COUNTY KILDARE *One of the world's great theological institutions, Maynooth stands on the site and ruins of Fitzgerald Castle, home of the once mighty Norman-Irish Geraldine family.*

ONE HUNDRED AND ELEVENTH SUCCESSOR TO
ST. PATRICK

Belfast-born Cardinal William Conway personifies the old guard. While publicly decrying the violence, he has done poor little to provide either inspiration or leadership to Northern Ireland's embattled Catholics.

A master at theological word games, he remains vague on most new issues while imposing a dogmatic hard line on old ones.

Heavily subsidized by the British government in operating sectarian public schools, he has remained insensitive to the need to get on with the integration of Protestant and Catholic children. Without this first step there is a virtual guarantee of the continuation of religious bloodshed in the next generation.

On such matters as mixed marriages, when the Vatican took a relaxed position, Cardinal Conway chose to interpret it in such a manner as to make it just as difficult and obnoxious for parents and children as before.

This combination of doctrinaire behavior and elusiveness has done little to speed up desperately needed progressive reform.

ALLIHIES *Her copper mines long played out, this town at land's end on the Bere peninsula tenaciously clings to life.*

3. A MYSTIC LAND AND SEASCAPE

Ireland has been described as a rather plain picture encased in a beautiful frame. This is mostly but not entirely true. Her coast, particularly in the southwest, offers up a haunting array of scenery. The Bere, least toured but most spectacular of the peninsulas, showed herself to be an eerie beauty of the mists, especially suited for the ghosts and fairies who live there.

LITTLE SKELLIG ISLAND

Eight miles at sea off the Ring of Kerry, this rock houses one of the most enthralling bird sanctuaries in the world. The majestic gannet grows to a wing span of six feet. Fishing for its prey, the gannet puts on a wild show, climbing to a height of a hundred feet, then plunging straight down, wings tucked, hitting the water at a great velocity, and coming up on the fish from below.

GOUGANEBARRA—County Cork

A natural basin for rain has created this lovely oasis in an otherwise desolate area. Source of the river Lee, it was the location of a monastic center founded by Finnbarr, the patron saint of Cork. The variety and species of its forest make this national park a unique jewel on the tree-starved Irish landscape.

MULRANY—County Mayo

Screened by barrier hills from the Atlantic, low tide in Clew Bay depicts an unusually tranquil climate.

Clare Island on the horizon houses the main fortress of Grace O'Malley, "Pirate Queen of Connaught." 'Tis said of Grace she brooked no guff at all from Elizabeth of England, who tried unsuccessfully, by bribe and threat, to get her to keep her hands off British shipping.

No Irish are more Irish than the O'Malleys of County Mayo. They are also nearly unique among Irish, with a tradition as seafarers.

A hellcat of the first order, Grace O'Malley devoured and discarded an inordinate number of husbands and lovers. Because she was the most Irish of the Irish, the fables about Grace would stagger the mind of even the most dedicated and believing Gaelophile.

She has been accorded a most unusual honor in that her Gaelic name, Gráinne Ni Mháille, is one of the symbolic names of Ireland itself.

REMORSELESS

Wind, fog, sea, and craggy rock crescendo on the Bere peninsula, wildest of Ireland's wild moors, giving testimony to the mysticism and cruelty of the land.

AFTER THE STORM
Gouganebarra National Park

DONEGAL *Between Bloody Foreland and Lettermacaward. A gentler coast, a veritable fairyland of dunes and coves, of glorious strands and caves, and no end of wonderful climbing rocks.*

WICKLOW MOUNTAINS, COUNTY WICKLOW *A sudden wee waterfall weaves its way down into the Vale of Glenmacnass and onto the monastic city of St. Kevin in Glendalough.*

BANTRY BAY

The very name conjures up an image of romance of the sea. This magnificent inlet has been the object of poem and song by many a fair waiting maiden and her lonely longing sailor boy. Likewise, it played host to more than one historical occasion. A French fleet set sail in 1796 with Wolfe Tone aboard to come to the aid of the United Irishmen's Uprising. Gales at sea scattered the fleet and a mere handful of the original number limped into Bantry Bay. A continuing storm sent them packing home, bringing the expedition to total failure.

CONNEMARA LUNARSCAPE—County Galway

Known in part as "Joyce Country," this perennially depressed area is a masterpiece of bleakness. Endless bogs and moors are crisscrossed by the lumpiest, waviest, most pocked roads in Ireland. It is the heartland of the Gaeltacht, and the ancient language is universally spoken.

The biggest news in these parts since Grace O'Malley is the Connemara pony. Steeds that arrived with the Celts were as crossbred as the Celts themselves. The ancestry of the Celtic pony can be traced, with accuracy, to the original wild horse of the Ice Age twenty thousand years ago.

Part of the Spanish Armada was wrecked on the Galway coast, dumping ashore Spanish warriors and their Andalusian horses. Andalusians, a cross of native Spanish and the Barb from Morocco, ran with the native herds.

At the beginning of the nineteenth century the Arabian was imported and infused, resulting in the Connemara pony.

Powerful and carefully bred, the Connemara pony works the land, races in his own circuit, hunts beautifully, is a splendid riding horse, and is most famous as a show jumper.

THE RING OF KERRY *The sea shows off those deep azure tones that could only mean one thing. Surely, it's solid . . . "Kerry blue."*

BERE PENINSULA

Much of the desolation is man-made. Although Ireland has always been sparse in trees, the word "derry" occurs in place names in many parts of the country, indicating a former stand of oaks.

The British cut down and carted off timber indiscriminately for their own consumption. This was part of a deliberate plan to denude the land in order to flush out the "woodkerns," those troublesome mobile bands of forest men.

Destruction of the trees not only had its obvious effects in soil erosion and on the watershed, but ended a woods culture that can only be recalled in peasant folklore.

SUNSET ON THE RIVER SHANNON

(Following page)
DONEGAL PASTORAL *Ancient patterns of the rundale system of land division still persist. The Inishowen peninsula, once part of the O'Neill clan pale, marks the northernmost part of the country.*

THE CONFRONTATION

4. THE SPORTING SCENE

In their island isolation the Celts necessarily invented their own unique games, the most Irish of which is hurling. The epic poem *The Cattle Raid of Cooley* is regarded as somewhat of an Irish Iliad. In this pre-Christian story we find reference to hurling by Cuchulain, the hero, who is a wizard with the caman, the hurling stick.

Legends about Finn McCool, after whom the Fenians are named, date back to A.D. 200. Among other notable feats, he lifted a rock out of Ulster and flung it into the ocean, thereby creating the Isle of Man. The hole it left is now Lough Neagh. During a hurling match, Gráinne, betrothed to Finn, has an eye on the hurler Diarmuid. It seems that Diarmuid owns a magic "love spot" on his forehead. No maiden who saw it could resist him. She saw it and she went the way of all flesh. Needless to conclude, it was Diarmuid's last match.

Along with the risky practice of putting ashen clubs in the hands of opposing Irishmen, other unique Gaelic games include camogie (women's hurling), Gaelic football and handball, and road bowling.

It follows that all these were forbidden by the British at various times in the past—as early as 1550. During penal days, secret mass was often followed by secret hurling matches be-

tween parishes, with up to two hundred men on each side. Death and dispersion caused by the famine all but destroyed these games.

In 1884 there was a startling revival with the formation of the Gaelic Athletic Association under Dr. Croke, the Archbishop of Cashel.

Michael Cusack, co-founder of the GAA and a County Clare-born Dublin schoolteacher, was the model for "The Citizen" in Joyce's *Ulysses*. It was Cusack who envisioned the revival as an integral part of nationalism, to fire up Irish pride in their own and to vanquish so much of the physical apathy. "Foreign games," meaning anything non-Gaelic, were first scorned, then later merely tolerated in a show of left-handed arrogance as the GAA became an important force.

Ireland is a renowned sportsman's valhalla. Everything is played and everything is bet on. Teams represent her in nearly all conventional international sports. Players and tourists flock to her streams and golf courses and racecourses. The major Anglo games of soccer football and rugby carry national teams, and other Anglo sports such as cricket, the hunt, and the show horse have their followings.

All these take a back seat when it comes to the All-Ireland in Gaelic football and hurling before crowds of ninety thousand in Dublin's Croke Park, headquarters of the Association.

51

HURLING *Hurling is played on a "pitch" or field approximately a hundred yards wide and a hundred and eighty long, fifteen men on each side armed with hurleys whale away at a leather ball. Brain and brawn are needed in equal measure with spellbinding displays of footwork in perfect co-ordination with stickwork. Two halves of thirty minutes go nonstop, with three substitutions allowed for the injured, who are dragged off the field. On this day it was Kilkenny, the Leinster Champs, over the Munster Champions from Rebel Cork.*

GAELIC FOOTBALL

Not as ancient but equally popular, this sport combines the best elements of most field sports. Often mistaken for a combination of rugby and soccer football, the Gaelic game predated the introduction of these sports by several centuries.

Swifter and wider open than rugby, it contains thunderous body contact, absent from soccer, while the leaps are reminiscent of basketball rebounding. Delicate hand and knee work barely keeps it on the sane side of mayhem. Played in two forty-minute periods without a time out, in the twilight mo-

ments a close game usually goes to the lads who declined the last glass of Guinness the night before.

These two splendid sports are played strictly for the glory, the GAA being completely amateur. Money earned is poured back into national programs, and there are hundreds of thousands of everyday participants.

The fans at Croke Park watched the lads from County Offaly battle Kerry to a tie in the All-Ireland.

HIND IS FORE, A BOB OR TWO!

Road bowling is rarely played outside the two widely separated counties of Armagh and Cork. Having no such niceties as alleys or greens when the game was founded, the participants took to the country roads. Today it is played where traffic is apt to be light and bowlers and car drivers are compatible with each other. Today's macadam surfaces are faster and trickier, making the game one of more skill.

A course can run up to several miles, the simple object being to advance the ball over the finish line in the least number of tosses. What is tossed is a "bullet" of solid cast iron weighing twenty-eight ounces.

The course is set up and down grades, around bends, and sometimes with such obstacles as rail bridges and streams. In the throwing there is an elaborate windup and run to mark, then flinging the "bullet" underhanded. All sorts of body English must be used to apply top spin, under spin, and curves to make the ball follow the course.

"Hind is fore, a bob or two," simply means, "I'll lay a bet that the trailing ball will be ahead after the next throw."

HAPPINESS IS . . .

IT'S THE DRAG

Ingenuity abounds in local and regional pastimes, all of them laced with the wager. Thousands of spectators and betting men from Cork and thereabouts descend on Kinsale for the All Ireland Drag. Bookies hawk odds in the main street while knowledgeable breeders and mere canine lovers inspect the hounds and study past records with all the seriousness of picking a Derby winner.

Bets down, the crowd moves en masse to a field outside town where a seventeen-mile course has been set by "dragging" scented meat irresistible to the beagles, who have been kept a bit on the slender side. The prize, a purse of £35. Obviously the big money is to be made with the bookmaker.

With a clean start assured by the sportsman judges, the pack breaks for the woods, returning the better part of an hour later gasping and weaving under desperate pleading of the owners to stagger over the finish line, somehow.

There then follows a universal exodus to the pubs to discuss what went right and what went wrong. That is, except for a dozen-odd owners who have lost dogs in the woods. Thereupon, an unscheduled game called "hunting for the beagle" may well go into the night.

LORD KILLANIN—WORLD SPORTSMAN *One of Ireland's most prominent international representatives, he is a prolific man. His board memberships and cultural and philanthropic activities cover the Irish spectrum. Associated with John Ford on* The Quiet Man *he has produced a number of his own films including* The Playboy of the Western World. *His co-authored guidebook on Ireland is the best of its species.*

A lifelong sportsman, boxer and crew at Cambridge, he presides over the Connemara Pony Breeders and the Galway Race Track.

In 1972, after two decades of service, he succeeded Avery Brundage as president of the International Olympic Committee.

JOHN MORRIS *Photographer son of Lord Killanin, he participated in an ornithological first in the successful breeding of the saker to the peregrine, making it the rarest falcon on earth.*

A dedicated falconer, he founded the Irish Hawking Club.

THE GALWAY RACES

5. THE LAND AND THE PEOPLE ARE ONE—The Dying West

The old man trudged down the path flanked on either side by omnipresent stone walls. Stone was everywhere, slicing up and enclosing infertile fields. Half the plots were stone slabs. Great rock shelves stepped down to the sea. Not a tree was in sight. The old man stopped. We greeted each other and talked awhile.

"Too bad there isn't a market for stone," I said.

He smiled. "Ah, if it was worth anything at all, the British would have carted it away a long time ago."

If sheer beauty were a measure of wealth, the west of Ireland would be one of the richest places on earth. Only part of this beauty lies with the overpowering coast, the cliffs, the lushness of green, and the high lakes. The other beauty, the inner and truth of beauty, are those people who have lived, labored, and suffered here. They are the gentle beauty of Ireland, soft and unsophisticated yet so full of wisdom and so dogged. They are the backbone of the race.

After all the struggle and bloodshed over land, after all the wars and risings and all the brutal toil, the end has been in vain. The Republic itself acts out a queer role in the demise of the West. They speak the new vernacular of consolidation and mechanization and industrialization. The EEC is hungry for Irish cattle, and conditions were never better for the continental investor. Moreover, there is no longer a feasible way for the small farmer to survive.

When the land began to quit, even the strongest were unable to continue. It really started with the coming of the tractor and the beginning of the consumer society, which forced more of the strong to abandon their farms and left more of the weak behind.

Many of those who stayed without land of their own were simply too debilitated to go. They became the doddering aunt and uncle living off a dole of a few pence a day in the most miserable sorts of hovels. Twenty per cent of the peasants remained lifelong celibates with the alcoholism and schizophrenia running hundreds of percentiles over their counterparts in other countries. Somehow, they hung on.

It has now fallen to them to be the last great peasantry of Western Europe. Their own lores and language are in their keeping as are the ancient customs of all those previous civilizations which made inroads.

After a fifty-year battle, Ireland is determining that resurrection of the old tongue is a lost cause. Only in the West is Gaelic the spoken and written word.

Always the most impoverished section of the country, it is continually being drained of young people. There is some hope that Ireland can reverse the emigration trend but the coming generations will want to live in cities and work in the new industrial estates and count their blessings in TV sets and automobiles. In the West, the schemes to industrialize simply haven't turned the tide.

In fact the West is a millstone around the nation's neck. Shedding her own agrarian mentality, Ireland is moving on an irreversible course into the world of the computer and the superhighway. The Irish will join a sort of European "unisex" and become not so different and apart from other people.

Yet, so long as no cloverleafs by-pass the villages, those harsh hillside plots and all the arduous life that goes with it remain in plain sight. The persistent bond of farm and farmer can be annoying. They wish the West wouldn't take so long to die. In truth, the West is the Irish conscience. When it goes, so much of what is great about being Irish will go with it.

THE STRAND, GLENBEIGH, COUNTY KERRY

Look on my thin grey hair and hollow cheeks
And on these hands that may not lift the sword,
This body trembling like a wind-blown reed.
No woman's loved me, no man sought my help.

"Fergus and the Druid,"
from *The Rose*, by
William Butler Yeats

THE DREAMER

CROSSROADS FROM NOWHERE TO NOWHERE

THE LAST WATER WHEEL
MILLTOWN, COUNTY KERRY
*Defying all attempts to purchase or
remove it, one of the last two or
three water wheels in Ireland powers
a sawmill.*

STRAW BOYS *and wren boys constitute a perfect example of
the peasant tradition of mummering finding its way to Ireland.
The cone-shaped hat is leprechaun wear, while the steeple hat
was used as a helmet in mock battles. Straw boys made their
appearance on St. Brigid's Day and All Saints' Eve and those
other occasions when the "little folk" were on the prowl. Posing
as "shipwrecked sailors," they crashed many a wedding, and
woe to the bride who refused them in dance.*

Today they are only seen in folk cultural gatherings.

THE LAST FAIR—UPPER CAMP, COUNTY KERRY *Contemplation, camaraderie and conversation that marked the traditional gatherings are fading quickly from the scene. Sheep judging was a serious business. A prize specimen often meant the difference between a good and a bad year.*

69

THE TINKERS

The origin of these wanderers is vague. Few are of Romany or gypsy stock. It is reasonable to assume they became displaced itinerants from all the land evictions, the Cromwell exile west of the Shannon, and penal times.

For centuries they have traveled given circuits in horse-drawn caravans plying the trade of "whitesmiths" or tin metal-workers, selling at fairs and doing fix-ups in the villages. They were in particular demand for building and servicing moonshine stills, which brewed a homemade concoction known as poteen.

Tribal in social structure, they abide by a rigid family code, gathering at annual celebrations such as the Puck Fair in Killorglin, which pays mock homage to a goat god.

The travelers, as they wish to call themselves, are obviously objects of farfetched tales and superstitions, many of which stem from a "magic" prowess as horse traders and occasional horse rustlers.

At the bottom of every health and educational statistic, they survive in abominable conditions, receiving more than their fair share of short life expectancy and of death through disease and infant mortality. Drinking, thievery, brawling, and begging are offshoots of a life of roaming in endless circles.

The "free" and uncluttered romance of sleeping under starry skies has little appeal to them, and efforts to establish permanent settlements are proving successful. Down to a few thousand, the dilapidated caravans may disappear from the scene, but the secret language and mystic ties will remain part of the Irish story forever.

GENERATIONS

THE ROMANCE OF TURF

No one who has left the shores of Eire will ever forget the blissful scent of the peat fire.

During a prehistoric era several thousand years before Christ, it is believed the forests were destroyed by a long reign of arctic weather. Though the trees fell, they did not decay through normal bacteriological processes, because of the cold wet climate. This accumulation of nondisintegrated trees and other plant life is the genesis of the bogs that cover some ten per cent of the Irish surface.

A turf culture can be traced back almost as far as human habitation of the island. Prime farm land was always dependent on the proximity to a bog.

The turf harvest has been an annual ritual for the peasant and communal existence at its most basic level. Each spring, when the first crop was in, the entire male population made to the bog where clamping, stacking, and drying were achieved as a village effort. Special barrows and conveyances, slanes and spades and other tools made it a way of life of its own. In the West, turf is still dug and cut by hand.

Today, an Irish Turf Board harvests some three million tons annually from midland bogs by advanced mechanical methods. Although it contains only half the potency of coal, turf provides the fuel for a quarter of the nation's electricity. Another two million tons go into the production of briquets for home consumption and peat moss. At the present rate of use, it is estimated there is still enough left for five hundred years.

Some bogs run as far down as fifty feet and have collected a chronological catalogue of animal and vegetable fossils, giving a windfall to the botanist and archaeologist.

Turf and Ireland go together with the potato and the Catholic Church. Between them, the Irish have been fed and kept warm physically and spiritually.

THE LAND AND THE PEOPLE ARE ONE 75

AN CLOCHAN—The Steppingstones

Clifden is appropriately named, for this is a sudden touch of Switzerland rising out of the desolate scenery.

It is the unofficial capital and home of the Connemara Pony Show, its main claim to fame being that Alcock and Brown landed here in 1919 in man's first flight across the Atlantic Ocean.

CONNEMARA

AN IRISH PARADOX

Young Fisherman—Castletownbere

She is an island without a tradition of the sea. There is virtually no navy or merchant marine and, until this century, no fishing industry.

Uncounted numbers starved during the famine because of ignorance of how to harvest the sea. Until recent years fish was scorned as "famine food," trash that the poor ate or that, at best, was consumed once a week on Friday. The lordly lobster itself and all those mussels and clams and oysters generally wound up in French bouillabaisse.

Nowadays the bountiful waters are heavily fished. Speaking again in the new vernacular, huge schemes are under way for artificial seeding and harvesting along the coastal waters, as well as inland hatcheries. Warm Gulf Stream currents and an exceptional condition of sheltered inlets give these experiments feasibility, and so Ireland in the future may well be a source of seafood for the Continent.

The Fleet—Killybegs

A poet in a land of poets, the Kerryman can be strange and distant. The Kerry girl may stare moody and pensive at the sea for hours, then suddenly burst out in a wild race down the strand against the last fit of sunlight.

Where village road meets the highway the neighbors meet and wait for the milk collection truck as they did yesterday and will do tomorrow.

A Traditional Threesome, Anyroad Ireland

A DYING WEST

The country fairs and all their blazing color have all but vanished before the marketing co-operatives. Songs and dances that once filled a midsummer's night are mostly sung in tourist taverns. Gone is the wandering scholar who kept the old lore and language alive in hedge schools. And soon the lanes and the horse carts and the stone walls will fade from the sight of the traveler, who will speed through on wide straight roads, and there will be neatly planned housing developments and shopping centers.

Once upon a time, when a family emigrated, the neighbors kept the turf fire "smoored" and burning for the day they would return. It is said that "once the fire goes out, the house will soon come tumbling down." In those savagely poor and humble little cottages the fires are going out all over the West and the voices of the gentle people will be heard no more. Surely it is a new day, but when the land loses its peasantry the beat of its heart is never the same again.

"Have yourself a good look now, for when I'm gone you'll never see the likes of a man like me, again."

6. DUBLIN'S FAIR CITY

"In Dublin's fair city,
Where the girls are so pretty,
I first set my eyes on sweet Mollie Malone."

The column honoring Horatio Nelson has been blown down and other offensive monuments praising "strangers" and "foreigners" have been removed. Streets and parks have been renamed after Irish patriots. Nonetheless Dublin remains a British hybrid.

Resembling a provincial capital more than the seat of government of a great republic, it doggedly keeps one foot in the last century, battling the dubious benefits of modern progress. The only world-class boulevard runs but a few blocks. One would be hard pressed to find many of the trappings of grand stature that usually go with a national capital.

Dublin manages to retain a refreshingly relaxed pace and atmosphere. It is an intimate city where everyone knows everyone and almost no one dresses well. Snobbery is nonexistent. It is a soft city with abundances of green and without the harsh fingers of skyscrapers. The people are the most polite in the world, and the random taxi driver can charm the spots off you quoting Joyce. The restaurants and cuisine are far better than one has been led to believe. Public buildings are on the lean side of grandeur but do command authority.

It is a man's city, lusty in a masculine way, with the throb of it centered in a cornucopia of pubs and sporting events.

Steeped mightily in history, Dublin is one of the few cities of its age to live its greatest moments of glory in this century.

First mentioned in A.D. 140 by the Macedonian Ptolemy, he gave it the name "Eblana," which still is seen on signs dangling over a few shops.

In 871 the Norsemen under Olaf the White established a walled town called Dubh Linn, the Black Pool, on a site south of Tara. His successor, Ivarr the Boneless, consolidated the kingdom and gave it its beginning as a world port and its entrance into the Viking era.

Established as the capital by the Normans, Dublin came out of the Middle Ages fairly well clawed up, dilapidated and badly depopulated by a recurring tale of fire, plague, and rebellion.

Beginning around 1700 with the reigns of four King Georges, it took on the Georgian character that identifies it today. Built for the comfort of the rulers and their Ascendancy, it was a decent place to live, close enough to England to acquire sophis-
(Continued on page 86)

tication and a drawing-room society. The rash of great public buildings assured the smooth administration of a feudal colony.

For those staggering masses of Catholics at the other end of the spectrum, Dublin was a deplorable hellhole embodying the worst conditions, such as marked the urban cesspools of that age.

A final rising evicted the overlords in 1916. The captains and the kings departed but left those ghosts that all Irishmen see at one time or another.

Dublin is probably as much a state of mind as any place in the world. It is ideas and visions and billions of words argued, in the glow of dark mahogany and stained glass enveloped by the scent of ale, by men with bottomless thirst for Guinness, Paddy, and conversation. Its Irishness is of the rarest genre, the kind that identifies Paris as French and Cheyenne as a cow town. What is more, no city anywhere can match the manner in which Dublin won its spurs—through men of letters and men of insurrection.

THE CASTLE

Bedford Tower, above the former Office of Heralds, now houses the Genealogical Office.

The Irish writer Sean O'Faolain made the following pointed observation about the role of the Castle in the history of his nation:

Dublin Castle had become the center of a softly purring machinery. It was to remain so until 1916. Unable to rule directly, the middle classes and gentry now had to persuade, influence, calm and coax the native millions, if necessary to buy

and bribe them with offices, jobs, favors, honors and above all by pure undiluted snobbery. With a minute garrison of British troops and a large *native* police force, The Castle did its job beautifully. Dublin's men of property persuaded or purchased, bamboozled or bullied, played ball almost to a man. It was one of the nicest examples in history of quiet colonial rule by use of the kid glove and the tinkling purse.

Unfortunately, a great deal of this mentality has lingered on in the bureaucracy.

THE FOUR COURTS

Thomas Cooley and James
Gandon are credited with the
lion's share of the public
buildings which sprouted up
at the end of the eighteenth
century. Begun by the former
and completed by the latter,
the Four Courts on Inns
Quay stands stately on the
banks of the river Liffey.

When it was seized by
Anti-Treaty forces in 1922,
the interior was badly
damaged. The restored
building houses the barristers'
law library and a number of
registries, as well as the
Supreme and High Courts.

The original four courts—
Exchequer, King's Bench,
Chancery, and Common
Pleas—fathered the British
character of Irish law, which
scarcely differs today.

The distinguishing feature
of Georgian Dublin is
fan-shaped transoms over
wildly colored doors with
the brass polished to a fare
thee well.

Least imposing of the ten spans that cross the Liffey, the Half-penny Bridge, left, no longer collects the toll for which it was named, but still carries a full complement of foot traffic over the river.

Christ Church Cathedral, right, dates back to 1038, built by the Norse King of Dublin on a site where Patrick preached. Strong-bow's effigy guards the tomb of the Norman conqueror. It was extraterritorial for Catholics for centuries, until Dr. Dermot Ryan, Archbishop of Dublin, ended the boycott with a visit in 1973, the first since the Reformation.

Completed in 1791, the Custom House, left, is considered Gandon's masterpiece. It is set majestically on a small bend in the Liffey as it makes its way from central Dublin to the bay. The interior was razed during the Civil War in 1921. Like most of the important buildings of the era, it has been restored and is in full use.

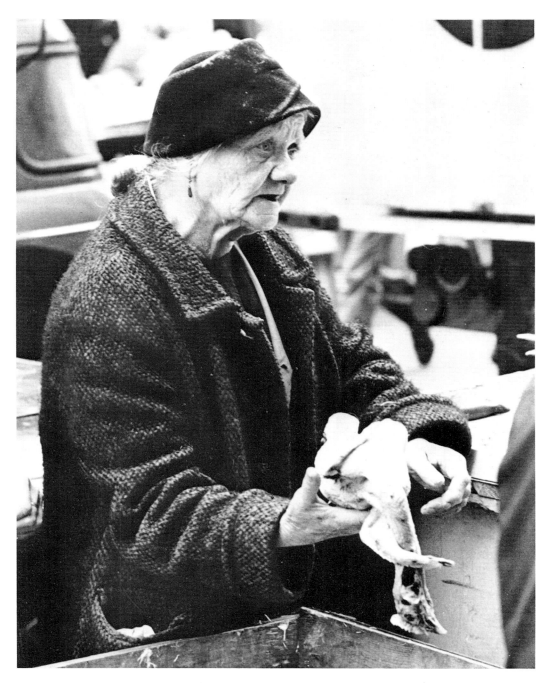

THE MOORE STREET MARKET

TUNING THE PIPES

Bagpipes in one form or another are indigenous to just about every European country, mostly as an instrument identified with shepherding and village dancing. In addition, Irish and Scottish pipes are an integral part of the regal and military music of clan and sept and regiment.

The piper here tunes up by bouncing a few notes off the wall.

BARD

THE LIBERTIES

The most ancient part of Dublin encompasses the Castle, the two cathedrals, and the core of the Viking and medieval cities. During the Georgian era it fell from grace to squalor. Those who did not toil for the Ascendancy existed in the abysmal night shelters after the "Penny Dinner." Overcrowding, filth, crime, hunger, and disease infested the area. It was the womb that bore the revolutionaries of generation after generaton.

Now redeemed as a workingman's district, it is closely tied to the huge Guinness Brewery. A Liberties Association has closed ranks to preserve its historical greatness and halt the planned encroachment of the bulldozer and all that follows in its wake.

AH, GUINNESS! *More than a brew, more than a meal, it is a culture, a cult, a way of life.*

In a tavern more resembling a German beer hall than an Irish inn, a modern version of balladeering is canned and served up nightly to the tourist bus trade.

ST. STEPHEN'S GREEN

TRINITY

Founded by Queen Elizabeth in 1591, the college was established to assure that the Ascendancy would receive a higher education without infection from all the popery about. A distinguished roll includes the dramatists Synge and Wilde and writer-philosophers Swift, Goldsmith, and Burke. Although Elizabeth certainly didn't plan it that way, a small legion of Irish patriots were educated at Trinity. Among their number, Robert Emmet, Henry Grattan, Thomas Davis, Isaac Butt, and Theobald Wolfe Tone. Edward Carson, one of the founders of Northern Ireland, attended.

The Library is the nation's largest and houses the most important collection of historical data. An eighth-century illuminated gospel book, the Book of Kells, is the most valuable in Ireland. The museum contains a harp somewhat questionably attributed to Brian Boru, which has become the symbol of Ireland.

Today the school has a coeducational student body from all religions. Its unusual setting in central Dublin and its college-town serenity do much to tone down the hustle and bustle swirling around it.

94

WORDS AND THE IRISH

The Irish love affair with words goes back to the dawn of her history. Fertile Celtic minds, filled with mysticism and fantasy, created a great inventory of legends. Chanted by Druid priests, they were passed down orally. Later the Celtic poet or *file* was trained in his art for years and held in esteem as nowhere else in the world.

St. Columba became the first great poet of record, father, sponsor, benefactor, and defender of the legion of poets.

In monastic cities production of manuscripts by scribes was carried on with the fervor of a waterfall. The Old Irish oral meanderings were updated and set down as written literature. This boundless wealth of material formed the cornerstone of the tradition.

W. B. Yeats, for example, wrote five plays based on the adventures of the legendary hero Cuchulain. "The Story of Deirdre" from the Book of Leinster has been the basis of classical romance and tragedy in countless modern works.

The Cattle Raid of Cooley, the Yellow Book of Lecan, stories of the Fenian cycle, and thousands of others transcribed by monks built the library, showing the beauty, Irish wit, and satirical penetration that throws out words with the deftness and power of a padded triphammer.

"Bard" is a Celtic word. During the Norman period, bards became attached to the aristocracy, receiving high status after a six-year course of study. The Irish bard became so politically caustic that the Statutes of Kilkenny outlawed him as well as the wandering balladeer.

The Reformation, conquest, and Penal Laws brought on a dark age to the Old Irish. During much of this period, Gaelic was forbidden and the stories as well as the religion were carried on orally. Keeping the Old Irish culture alive fell to the storyteller. In every village and situation he was the man of stature just below the priest.

Illiteracy became universal. People learned to think without sight of the written word. This did much to sharpen mental agility, so that thoughts into words were honed to a diamond-edge quality. With English as the imposed language, English was embellished and enriched, making Irish/English a tongue of its own with a quality of its own.

Something of the Old Irish must have rubbed off on the Ascendancy, which produced a brilliant line of writers. Ascendancy nationalists in the Wolfe Tone era and afterward kept a certain quality alive with pamphleteering and speeches from the dock.

A literary revival burst out at the end of the nineteenth century on the wings of patriotic fervor. Dublin became the center of the voluminous outpourings.

Yet, at the bedrock level of this revival, the giants of the day found their way by treading the paths of ancient glory.

Much of the revival was bitterly anti-Catholic. A writer must be as free as the man who longs for liberty, and clerically inspired prudishness made the air too stifling. Two of the titans, James Joyce and Sean O'Casey, went into self-imposed exile, a tragic fate that most Irish writers would have to follow.

Why do the Irish write? Because they need weapons, and an island without a navy has poor few of them. Surely, the use of words has been the most powerful weapon in the Irish arsenal.

Doldrums and a sense of despair have descended on the scene. Nowhere are so many books and plays talked about that are never written. Still, you have a feeling that the lads are just catching their breath. Certainly Belfast is never going to replace Dublin as one of the world's literary Meccas, but the next great round of writing is destined to come out of the suffering in the North.

THE ABBEY—Ireland's National Theater

"We propose to have performed in Dublin, in the Spring of every year, certain Celtic and Irish plays which, whatever their degree and excellence, will be written with a high ambition and so build up a Celtic and Irish school of Dramatic Art. . . ."

Thus wrote Lady Gregory, Edward Martyn, and young William Butler Yeats in launching what was to become one of the landmark undertakings in the history of the stage.

The dramatist and the player have blended in what has proved to be a game of words in which the Irish have no peers. As small and limited in resources as the Irish population may be, this manner of expression has reached a human zenith in Dublin.

Tomas Mac Anna, producer and director of the Abbey, oversees a rehearsal of Brian Friel's Philadelphia, Here I Come!, *the most acclaimed Irish play of recent years.*

McDAID'S

The old pub on Harry Street had stood for a hundred and twenty-five years. It had been a literary hangout for poets and critics and actor folk and more than one tirade from the Brendan Behans of the day. McDaid's came on hard times and the closing notice had to be posted.

A Dubliner entered for a last sentimental cup. Strewn about the place were those "literary" lights who had called it a second home. In various states of decomposition, one was out cold with his face on the bar, another was glassy-eyed with runny nose to match, and yet another, a poet, mumbled his last published work incoherently; the one he had written twenty years ago.

Surveying the human wreckage and thinking of the upcoming auctioneer's hammer, the observer opined, "It appears that the ship is deserting the sinking rats."

P.S. McDaid's lives!

THE DUBLINER

Students' haven—Respite in St. Stephen's Green

Rhododendron forest, right, in the grounds of Howth Castle, growing in a sheltered north slope on self-made peat. Perfect natural conditions make it one of the greatest rhododendron collections outside the Himalayas and China.

Dublin sunrise

7. REBEL CORK

The Bells of Shandon
That sound so grand
On the pleasant waters of the River Lee . . .

This nostalgic ditty by Corkonian Father Francis Mahony is an ode to the bells in the tower of that church of the other persuasion that have chimed over the city for two hundred and fifty years. The clock, younger than the bells, is called "The Four-faced Liar." During the hour each of the sides takes an independent route, but somehow they all end up together on the hour.

Cork, from the Gaelic word "Corcaigh," refers to the marshes on which the city is situated. The complex of canals and pilings is not unlike that of Venice. Although it is populated by only a hundred thousand people, one immediately gets the feel of a mercantile center, Hanseatic in tone, with a full complement of "merchant princes." A great natural harbor and the surrounding towns created a formidable naval presence, and the yachting set likewise made the environs of Cork the apple of the British eye; they did not give it back until 1938.

Cork men Frank O'Connor, Sean O'Faolain, and Daniel Corkery are certainly among the best of the modern writers. The undertone of wealth has patronized a respectable range of cultural pursuits, with ballet, theater, art, and music having quite good standards. An international film festival has circumvented Ireland's censorship and the local bishop's thunderous objections to the exposure of female flesh.

The Cork man owns a patented cutting humor and a natural distaste for Dublin or anything else nonCork. He is *the* sportsman in a land of sportsmen. His hurling team is a perennial power and contender, if not champion. He will play, and certainly bet on, anything that runs or any spheroid that is batted, kicked, or flung. He is a most generous supporter of the country's largest greyhound track.

Finnbarr is the saint of record. The city gets its name, "Rebel Cork," from the unfortunate circumstance of being on the wrong side in almost every war. But as the Corkonian says, "Once down is no defeat. We'll play them again with a bigger ball."

KINSALE, *left, site of Mountjoy's victory over the Irish and their Spanish allies in 1602, spelling the end of the Gaelic-Norman order. Marvelous sailing, deep-sea fishing, and a long presence reinforced by retired navy men have kept Kinsale as a quasi-British enclave. It is shared as a playground by the "merchant princes" of Cork.*

SUMMER COVE, *right. Deliciously old and quaint, just around the bend of the bay from Kinsale.*

COBH—HARBOR OF CORK, *left. Situated on the estuary of one of the world's great natural harbors, Ireland's port of call hosted the sailing of the first ocean-crossing steamer in 1838. It holds the grave of hundreds from the Lusitania, which was sunk nearby during World War I. Cobh also houses the oldest yacht club in the British Isles, a fact that is a somewhat diabolical play on the sorrow of those hundreds of thousands who emigrated from famine and destitution.*

CORK CRYSTAL *A famous old Cork craft undergoes a modern revival.*

Terence MacSwiney lies near Thomas MacCurtain among their comrades of the Cork Brigades in the IRA burial plot in St. Finnbarr's Cemetery.

Not least among the attributes of the Cork man is his reputation as a fighter, enhanced in the Rising of 1916. Michael Collins, most revered figure of the insurrection, was born a short distance from the city. The Cork Brigades of the IRA were among the most effective units fighting the British, particularly the Third, which played havoc with the Black and Tans by their "flying columns."

In the foyer of Cork City Hall two busts by the sculptor Seamus Murphy flank the main entrance, lionizing Thomas MacCurtain and Terence MacSwiney, martyrs of the rising.

MacCurtain, a Cork merchant, city alderman, and father of five, commanded the First IRA Cork Brigade. He was a decent and compassionate man, verging on greatness and dedicated to the Republican cause. By unanimous choice of his fellow aldermen he was elected the city's first Republican mayor in 1920. By taking the chain of office he assured an early death.

Thomas MacCurtain was murdered in his home before the eyes of his wife and children on his thirty-sixth birthday. A coroner's jury, jeopardizing their own lives, handed down the verdict that he had been willfully murdered by the Royal Irish Constabulary on instructions of the British government.

His successor, the writer and poet Terence MacSwiney, was likewise an ardent Republican and commander of the First Cork. Interned in Brixton prison in London, he commenced a hunger strike which epitomized Irish determination for freedom. The British were equally adamant and the strike dragged on for week after week, galvanizing world opinion. The death of MacSwiney after seventy-four days did much to break the British will. This Cork man was to leave behind suitable words for all of his breed who would follow: "It is not those who can inflict the most, but those that can suffer the most who will conquer."

Thomas MacCurtain's small clothing factory was on the ground floor of 40 Davis Street. Murder in the middle of the night by a pair of blackened gunmen took place in the living quarters above.

NO TWO LEAVES ARE ALIKE

Even when work was plentiful, the stone carvers who worked the cities and countryside were a small, exclusive club. After seven years' apprenticeship at virtually no pay, Seamus Murphy became the only true stone carver that Cork produced in twenty-five years. The son of Long Jim Murphy, a train engineer, he came up the route of poor Irish in a large family with no chance for a proper education. His native ability in art captured the attention of Daniel Corkery, who encouraged him through the Cork Art School by night classes.

The "stonies" are gone except for four in Dublin and Seamus in Cork. Romanesque buildings that they adorned mostly for the Church by hammer, mallet, and chisel have given way to glass, steel, and concrete boxes. Even the tombstones, the main support of the trade, have machine-carved lettering, and some of them aren't even of proper stone.

Seamus Murphy matriculated from poor "stonie" to poor sculptor. A single year in Paris, his only travel outside Ireland, established a set of standards. What he really learned, he learned as a boy by studying a leaf to carve a leaf. Little in life escapes his eye.

Ireland's greatest classical sculptor is a self-made genius, the sweetest human being ever to come our way. His studio is an unheated shack covered with corrugated metal, but inside there is a chronicle of Ireland's history in the twentieth century in a regiment of plaster busts. His wife, Maiyread, worries constantly over his visits to the hospital—twenty-two so far—for transfusions for a chronic ulcer condition. Seamus merely shrugs. "You'd think that after being in twenty-two times she'd know I'll be back for a twenty-third. . . .

"Art is an ordinary part of the life process," he says. "A person may do the same sort of work day in and day out. One day, by curious fortune, it may be done in a way it was never done before and you know you have created something. It may or may not be a work of art. On the other hand," he adds with a twinkle, "a lot of things that pass for art may well not be art at all."

No artist's haven this; it has been an unjust struggle without full due. It doesn't seem to matter, for this is a man who has never been at war with himself and finds inner riches from a piece of well-done work.

Rewards? "Knowing your own country by the uniqueness of each quarry. After all, stone carving is perhaps man's oldest profession. And then, there is something of mine in almost every city and town and it's made of stone and it will last. What more can a man want?"

The man is gone, but everyone and everything he touched remembers.

8. THE ISLANDS

A LOVELY TOUCH OF MADNESS

No one epitomizes the distant qualities of the Celt better than the man who inhabits the "mythical kingdom" of Kerry. Dreamer and poet, a bit wild and a bit mad. And once you know him, he's not all that cold an article.

Des Lavelle is the son of a traveling lighthouse keeper, born and raised on Valencia Island by a grandfather who was also a lighthouse man. On the cliffs of Bray Head, a clear day will reveal coast and open sea to the taunting pinnacles of the Skelligs. Even before his first visit at the age of nine he was steeped in their tales, which went back a thousand years before Christ. Dara Down, King of the World, rested out there in A.D. 200 before proceeding to Ventry to do battle with Finn MacCool, and the battle lasted for a year and a day.

Those pinnacled islands silently observed the march of history to Irish shores. They wrecked ships, hosted fleeing kings, housed a monastery, and quaked under Viking sackings.

For the casual observer, the Skelligs today may seem rather dead. The long-abandoned monastery, a lighthouse, and a gannet sanctuary on the small island. But ordinary people sometimes cannot see what is obvious to a less hurried Kerryman. Under the outward blandness of rock there exists a beat of life.

In Des's youth the boats didn't travel there often. One visit a summer was the highlight of his year. When he became a boatman he answered the beckoning call as often as he was able. Risking sheer precipices and a perilous sea approach to the Little Skellig, he has climbed and combed every inch, becoming en route a self-taught ornithologist, geologist, botanist, archaeologist, and historian. He has catalogued the changing robes of flowers from the early-blooming sea pinks to the late daisies, the nine species of snails and four of slugs that share an underworld with rabbits and field mice which are endangering the big island's underpinnings. He has restored old logs from the first lighthouse built on Skellig Michael a hundred and fifty years ago and studied them with the severity with which one would study the Book of Kells.

Mainly he has learned the life, habits, and travels of the cliff dwellers, those flocks of puffins and razorbills and shearwaters and guillemots and kittiwakes and petrels and gulls. On each visit there is always something new to be discovered.

Why does a man leave his wife and children ashore for these long periods of loneliness? Is he the counterpart of the desert man? Has it all to do with the Irish way? Or is he all that lonely, indeed? He does admit to possessiveness about the Skelligs and he does feel that a man works best alone.

"I go out there so I can look into myself, and when I'm there I can see myself standing still and the rest of the world going mad."

One evening Des's boat glided under the bridge connecting Valencia with Portmagee. We took a last look back to the islands. It suddenly occurred to me that he was the only man I've ever met who has an absolutely clear conception of heaven.

THE KERRYMAN

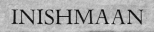

INISHMAAN

THE ARANS

At the mouth of Galway Bay three limestone plateaus rise from the sea, forming Inishmore, Inishmaan, and Inisheer and a most unusual mini-culture. The best guess is that they were populated by a tribe of Celts of Belgian origin seeking haven from defeat in battle. St. Enda converted them to Christianity in the fifth century, and they were not overlooked in Viking raids. In the Middle Ages the "Furious" O'Flahertys of Galway and the O'Brien sept of Clare were in constant battle over possession, but British conquest ended all that.

The Arans have long enticed writers seeking to purge the soot of civilization from themselves and bathe in the unmatched solitude. Liam O'Flaherty, author of *The Informer* and native of Inishmore, is her most famous son. John Millington Synge lived on Inishmaan, the setting of his *Riders to the Sea*.

On Inishmore, the large island, some trappings from the outside world are visible: a few dozen automobiles and telephones, a few miles of paved road, a small-craft landing strip seldom visited, and a handful of home-size electric generators in use for a couple of hours a day. An islander will tell you about the tidal wave that crashed ashore and climbed several hundred feet up the Inishmore cliffs, washing away a dozen fishermen. The description is so vivid and detailed you can scarcely believe that the event took place a hundred and fifty years ago. Indeed, time has stood still and life is quite the way it was.

What staggers the mind is how the people manage to cultivate anything. Soil is literally created by the bucketful—and fertilized by seaweed and hand-set in the crevices and enclosures. The complex rundale system of stone walls blocks potentially ravaging winds, while natural warmth is provided by the limestone. A meager crop is augmented by utterly dauntless fishermen who take to treacherous waters in those fragile little curraghs. The hand-knitted Aran sweaters once carried a distinctive pattern for each family so that a drowned fisherman or sailor who was washed up on the mainland could be identified.

The islanders will die harder than their brothers in the West. The Arans will be the final stronghold of the Celts. Many leave but many come back after taking their fling at the world beyond and all its confusion, shoving, and poverty. Others will work a life abroad until their pensions come due so that they can return. Those who go never get the sound of the sea from their ears or the sight of it from their dreams. They return to these forlorn rocks, for only here is there true peace.

DUN AENGUS *On the outer perimeter of the Celtic fortress which has been deemed to be among the half dozen great prehistoric antiquities of the Western world, a field of pointed limestones set upright formed a cheval-de-frise to slow down oncoming infantry; it was somewhat comparable to latter-day tank traps and barbed wire.*

AN INWARD BREED *After an hour and a half of total silence in the pub, the islander managed two words. "Dirty weather" is what he said and that was all he said. Defiant of their way of life and proud in their frugality, they keep the stranger at arm's length.*

The islander can read an outsider's thoughts with terse accuracy. You know you have it made when they invite you into their kitchen.

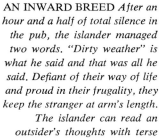

THE HERNONS OF KILMURVEY

Next to the sea the departed islander will remember the kitchen, the heart of his existence. A peat fire is always "smoored" and alive. With winters cold, wet, and seemingly eternal, there is no other heat or light in most of the homes. All the meals, the social life, the reading, the cottage industries come from this room.

Sonny Hernon works his field in a village where a goodly number of the people are Hernons. Brigid runs the island's most noted guesthouse with the authority of a lovable dictator. Her sharp tongue is known affectionately throughout Ireland by a legion of faithful who have found their way to Inishmore for a moment of serenity.

FATHER PAT

Pat O'Toole's dad lived in the States for eleven years before returning to his Aran sweetheart. Three of his brothers are American citizens. All seven of the children, except Pat, are in Inishmore to stay.

His beat was Nigeria in Godforsaken places where only an Irish missionary would go. Establishing schools, on loan from one station to another, he was finally gutted and felled by malaria and a host of jungle maladies.

He's a dogged man battling to regain his health so he can return. Father Pat's life commitment overrules any admission that he yearns for the sea. But wherever home was—an emir's palace or a sod hut miles from water—the wall held a crucifix and a single picture—of Inishmore and the sea.

117

A distinguished roll of wrecked ships testifies to the roughness of this coast. In the old days traffic to and from the mainland consisted of a fleet of small single-masted sailboats called "hookers." They are all gone now except for a few retained as sentimental keepsakes. Today a steamer from Galway services the Arans on a regular run.

Inadequate docking facilities on the two smaller islands force the ship to anchor offshore and move cargo by curragh. Pigs and sheep are hog-tied, sacked, and rowed out.

Cattle and horses pose a different problem. They are driven into the water by screaming women and children and dragged by lines to the ship, where a risky business follows in attaching animal to boom. It's a communal affair in which everyone gets soaked but with amazingly few mishaps.

SIDECAR *With Inishmore's one-automobile taxi fleet in perpetual motion, an alternate ride is hired by the time-honored jaunting car or sidecar, an Irish original.*

ARAN BEAUTIES

ANGELA

ANN

RANNY HERNON

BOLD MEN FACE SLASHING WATERS

A light and delicate homemade vessel has served in the wicked coastal waters since Celtic settlement. In ancient times, curraghs carrying up to two dozen men raided the English coast until, a millennium ago, Viking longboats swept them from the high seas.

The basic curragh is a basketlike lath frame covered by hide or tarred canvas. The entire craft and particularly the pointed nose ride high with almost no draft. Armed with a bottle of holy water, it is rowed by a cross-handed pull on a bladeless oar so that it literally glides over wave tops unaffected by currents. Some curraghs carry more than a ton. A basic mode of transportation, they convey cattle, crops, pigs, and passengers. Fishing is done from them by long line, nets, or pots; kelp is harvested for food and fertilizer, and sharks are hunted for oil.

Before the recent advent of rubber soles, Aran Islanders created special nonskid shoes for the wet rocks and curraghs exotically called "pampooties."

Carrownlisheen Townland—Inishmaan

Timeless, the thatched, whitewashed cottage, mortarless stone wall, and hay drying portray a centuries-old lifestyle.

122

Sunday Mass, Inishmore

Dun Conor, an oval dry-stone fort, caps the limestone slab of Inishmaan.

BOREDOM IS A
CAREFULLY
CULTIVATED
LUXURY
FOR SOME . . .

. . . BUT FOR OTHERS,
A RESTLESS CHURNING

The weekly ceilidhi begins when the pubs close; it is a conglomerate of old and new dances. The island priest hovers over the scene, a stern chaperon. Mostly, the boys sit on one side and the girls on the other. When the music begins, the boys cross over, grab up, and give it a heavy-footed whirl, then all return to their separate but equal sides.

For young people there is little respite from boredom. No movies, no TV, no hotels, no restaurants, no cars, no dance halls, and no place to rendezvous from the cold except for the kitchen fire, the most public place in the house.

Enough tourists and islanders have returned with tall tales of the outside world to evoke curiosity. Many islanders will leave. A lesser number will return to stay.

Sunset over Keel Township captures the instant of purple peculiar to the Achill sky.

ACHILL—One That Lived

Ireland's largest island is a short bridge hop over the sound. It was the home of the infamous British Captain Boycott, whose exploitation of and cruelty to peasant and worker brought on a countering refusal by them to work his lands. The tactic was so successful that his name became a word in the English language.

Most of the land is too hilly and boggy for successful farming. Ghost towns mark the failure and demise of the Catholic peasant.

An attempt was made early in the last century to establish an Ascendancy plantation. It is said that after they had grabbed the best land the Catholic priest put a curse on the insurgents. The Protestant community went semi-sterile, unable to produce sufficient heirs, and the venture ended in disaster and ghost towns of their own.

With a good share of western Irish scenery, and waters filled with accommodating fish and exquisite beaches, Achill has become a vital tourist attraction with a budding art colony.

130

THE BLASKETS—One That Died

The westernmost point in Europe, the Blaskets lie three miles off Slea Head on the Dingle peninsula. Hereabouts, St. Brendan, the navigator, was the pre-eminent force. Brendan and a dozen of his monks set sail through the Blaskets on the way to real or imagined discovery of America in the seventh century.

A fleet of curraghs was once ferried to the mainland, crossing a treacherous channel that has piled up ships from the time of the Armada on down through two World Wars. Flotsam and jetsam from these wrecks periodically augmented the meager income of the islanders.

The islands being Gaelic and medieval, the battle for survival was one of diminishing returns. Often the population doubled as the islands accommodated starving peasants fleeing the mainland. During the nineteenth century they declared themselves an independent republic in a futile attempt against the land agents.

As they floundered into the twentieth century, innumerable schemes were tried to settle and hold the Great Blasket. The banner was struck in 1957 and the island abandoned.

A small literary miracle in the form of three books has given the Blaskets a life beyond death. Maurice O'Sullivan's *Twenty Years A-growing,* Peig Sayers's *An Old Woman's Reflections,* and Tomas O Crohan's *The Islandman* are minor Gaelic classics.

Translated by the British Celticist Robin Flower, O'Crohan's memoirs open with a lilt of thought and language the likes of which are hardly seen any more.

I was born on St. Thomas's day in the year 1856. I can recall being at my mother's breast, for I was four years old before I was weaned. I am "the scrapings of the pot," the last of the litter. That's why I was left so long at the breasts. I was a spoilt child, too.

Four sisters I had, and every one of them putting her own titbit into my mouth. They treated me like a young bird in the nest. Maura Donel, Kate Donel, Eileen Donel, and Nora Donel those were their names. My brother was Pats Donel, and I am Tomas Donel. Maura is living still in this island, two of them are still alive in America, and Pats isn't dead yet. That was the whole bunch of us. They are all well grown when I was a baby, so that it was little wonder that I was spoilt among them all. Nobody expected me at all when I came their way.

At the close of the memoir in 1926, Tomas O Crohan ends his story prophetically.

I am old now. Many a thing has happened to me in the running of my days until now. People have come into the world around me and have gone again. There are only five older than me alive in the Island. They have the pension. I have only two months to go till that date—a date I have no fancy for. In my eyes it is a warning that death is coming, though there are many people who would rather be old with the pension than young without it.

I can remember being at my mother's breast. She would carry me up to the hill in a creel she had for bringing home the turf. When the creel was full of turf, she would come back with me under her arm. I remember being a boy; I remember being a young man; I remember the bloom of my vigour and my strength. I have known famine and plenty, fortune and ill-fortune, in my life-days till to-day. They are great teachers for one that marks them well.

One day there will be none left in the Blasket of all I have mentioned in this book—and none to remember them. I am thankful to God, who has given me the chance to preserve from forgetfulness those days that I have seen with my own eyes and have borne their burden, and that when I am gone men will know what life was like in my time and the neighbors that lived with me.

POST SCRIPT

In the early 1970s, Taylor Collings, a retired American industrialist of Irish descent, bought up most of the Great Blasket from heirs of families who had abandoned the island. He has established a sheep ranch in the teeth of a plague of rabbits and plans a small guesthouse with everything done in the old way. Collings is keenly aware of his historic responsibilities.

Although the island had been derelict for a decade and a half and although most were more than willing to sell, everyone knows there are ghosts out there and some think it best not to stir up ashes.

133

9. HER GREATEST RESOURCE

Indications are that Ireland has begun to reverse a hundred-and-twenty-five-year trend of emigration. It should not be taken for granted that the EEC is a cure-all or that economic betterment alone will hold the future generations. Reforms in working conditions and in health and social services will mend only part of the ills. Material gains must be matched, stride for stride, by the creation of a climate in which sharp young inquisitive minds can purge a holdover of spiritual poverty. There is a lot of stale air which the young people will refuse to breathe, a stagnation resulting from an antiquated, unreal, unnatural code of imposed morality.

As a subject race, the Irish have had much of their ambition knocked out of them. Those who hungered to achieve excellence were forced to do it "over the water." During British rule, a peasant who improved his land increased its value thereby and had his rent raised for his efforts. Penalizing someone who is trying to better himself has resulted in a "what's the use" attitude that has existed in part till today. It has invoked a state of mind in which the acceptance of the menial and the mediocre is commonplace. It has robbed the nation of families who would sacrifice heaven and earth to put sons through medical school. And what family in Ireland would push a daughter to any station above domestic, factory, or sales work? By way of example, a large contingent of Commonwealth Asiatics—Indians and Pakistanis—educated in London, serve in Ireland as physicians.

Once the Irishman accepted his low status, he began to opt out on life, longing for the simple ways, avoiding the rat race at any cost. There has been no large, vital middle class of professionals and skilled workers with a thirst for knowledge implanted, encouraged, and cultivated.

A long time ago, when Europe was mired in a dark age, Irish monks were afire with an insatiable drive for knowledge. When the literary revival came at the beginning of this century, the Irish writer drew from the deep well of heritage, using ancient glory as the foundation for the modern era.

Perhaps Ireland's outlook would be uncertain if the Irish were an ordinary people, but they are not. In every age of subjugation and agony they continued to turn out a full complement of brilliant men and women. Greatness is part and parcel of the Irish past, and it has only been tarnished, not diminished. They are easily identified as gifted and must use this ability to go after what is rightfully theirs and what is cer-

tainly within their reach. A kind of nepotism is required of the father working for his son's betterment rather than letting him set off for Australia. He must believe and work to the proposition that a good life and success can be attained in Ireland.

Paramount to any bright new dawn must be a reappraisal of the woman. That fabled green-eyed Irish colleen who transcends all loveliness and can smite a poor male's heart with a mere smile is the figment of some storyteller's imagination. The Irishwoman is the second-class citizen of the Western world. Functional plainness, even drabness, has been imposed on her by men who have been scared spitless over sex and marriage. Except for the odd travel poster, she finds very little encouragement to make herself lovely and attractive, because such efforts are hardly appreciated.

Irishwomen are certainly not in tune with the dizzying goals of the American feminist revolution, which is simply beyond comprehension. What is lacking is simple respect and dignity for a fellow human being. A woman who protests is apt to be branded as anti-God, and those few who have achieved

135

equal status through ability are regarded as freaks.

"Momism" and the avoidance of the "burden of marriage" have created a large body of men in the drinking brotherhood who are a bunch of overgrown boys. To them, masculinity is nothing more or less than physical prowess.

Eventually, even for them, someone has to replace Mom, and it will have to be that childbearing creature who must remain permissive of male superiority, allow the pub culture to continue, and then create a generation of "momism" of her own.

Her own fate has already been sealed early in life by the Jansenistic influence of the French priests who fathered modern Irish Catholicism at Maynooth. For the Hierarchy, fanatical in their repression of sex, no extreme was too great, even to making a woman bathe with clothing on to avoid the "mortal sin" of seeing her own naked body.

When this terrified young lady meets the terrified overgrown boy and both are aging rapidly, the result is a tragic institution known as the Irish marriage.

It has been glorified as a pillar and cornerstone of righteous existence, a perpetuation of godliness on earth and a great moral ethic. However, those who praise it the most consider celibacy a higher form of life than marriage.

The blissful couple, older than any of their European or American counterparts, enter a marriage where they must agree to preconditions and rules that start them out in a ten-foot

hole. It is no marriage of two, but of three, and the third is not so silent a partner.

After having done its bit to wreak havoc with normal sexual impulse, creating a devil of shame and guilt, the Church then joins the newlyweds in the bedroom, the one place on this earth that two people ought to be left alone. Indeed, Irish marriage can turn into a life sentence from which there is neither pardon nor parole, and that's a heavy reason why it is avoided as long as possible.

This sacred institution has been kept in an airtight chamber, away from scrutiny, as so much dirt swept under the rug or locked in the confessional. However, today, marriage Irish style is getting a long cold look, and the statistics on failure and the by-products of failure are horrifying in comparison to the rest of Western civilization. What has been unearthed is an abnormal toll of frigidity, desertions, alcoholism, mental disorder from despair and the misery of oversized families unable to survive whole.

Church dogma, backed to the hilt by Irish law, forbids the three things that could alleviate much of suffering—abortion, contraception, and divorce. In a recent court case an impoverished, deaf mute woman who had borne all the children she was physically capable of was charged with the crime of importing a contraceptive. When it was proved her life would

137

be endangered by further childbearing, the court suggested she and her husband continue life together as "brother and sister." It was to become a landmark case.

No marriage, no matter how dreadful, can be dissolved in Ireland, where a farce of "legal separations" is mushrooming. Divorce (rather, papal annulment) is a game that only the very rich can play after years of word trials and brazen payoffs in Rome. In upholding laws that infringe on basic human rights, the Irish courts often act more like medieval star chambers hunting witches and heretics.

Ireland is a land bursting with grand young people, who, if given their heads, will create a new nation of unsurpassed vitality and bestow on all men those very special gifts that are theirs alone to bestow.

The Irish have succeeded in a tortuous struggle to end the repression of the colonizer. They now stand at the threshold of defeating economic want.

The young people, her greatest resource, must be made to believe in themselves and be encouraged, even driven, by their elders to succeed in their own country. They must realize that

138

half the brain power belongs to women, and full, rich use of it will enhance everyone. They must turn back the most evil of all repressions, blind obedience that dulls the human mind and deflates the human spirit. They must learn that love is not a set of edicts. They must look, without shame, into the eyes of their women, and if they look deeply enough they might even find that mythical green-eyed colleen. They must come to know that love must be practiced in complete freedom and the human heart has no place for man-made canons of destruction.

Only a man and a woman can create the kind of life and the kind of country of their longing. Total marriage and not celibacy, indeed, is the highest form of human existence.

139

God willing, this will be Ireland's first generation in over a century to be able to remain in their own land.

THE
ETERNAL REPUBLICAN

In the post-famine era the quest for independence was stopped cold in the British Parliament and by armed forces in battle. Parnell was dead. One Home Rule Bill had been defeated and another vetoed in Lords. The Fenian rebellion of 1867 had been crushed. Yet it was to be a relic of that rising, Jeremiah O'Donovan Rossa, who was to play a peculiar role in the resurrection a half century later. Embers of Republicanism, dimmed to the faintest glow yet in all those little cottages and wretched hovels, smoored and ready to ignite like peat fires.

Groping for new direction and expression, the Gaelic Athletic Association made the first important inroad in 1884.

Ten years later an urbanized counterpart of the GAA, which attracted intellectuals, exploded on the scene. Founded by an Ulsterman professor, Eoin MacNeill, and Dr. Douglas Hyde, poet, playwright, and folklorist, the Gaelic League became the very womb of Republicanism. An arsenal of words was built with the stunning revival of the ancient tongue, so that Irishmen could draw strength, hope, and pride from their past. The League and the literary revival cannot be underestimated as catalysts of liberty, and it was only fitting that the poet Douglas Hyde—a Protestant, incidentally—should become the first President of the Irish Republic in 1937.

The outpouring of nationalistic literature reached an emotional crescendo with the presentation of Yeats's play *Cathleen Ni Houlihan,* the title itself a name for "Mother Ireland."

At the beginning of the twentieth century, John Redmond pulled together the remnants of Parnell's Irish Party, but the issue of home rule lay in limbo. However, the Irish Republican Brotherhood, direct descendants of the illegal Fenians, were regrouping and arming in secret.

The leadership of the clique of Republican intellectuals fell to Arthur Griffith, a political journalist who founded a newspaper, *The United Irishman,* using the name of Wolfe Tone's organization, which had staged a rising a century earlier. Disenchanted with Redmond's party and totally disbelieving British home rule promises, Griffith formed a new political party, Sinn Fein, in 1906. Sinn Fein, meaning "Ourselves Alone," was at first small and ineffectual and filled with dreamers, but at least the Republicans now had a political arm to move in concert with the Brotherhood. Sinn Fein was later to become the dominant political force during the insurrection and Griffith the first President of the Irish Free State.

In the British parliamentary election of 1910, the home rule issue was again paramount. John Redmond found himself in a tactical advantage used so brilliantly by Parnell, in that the Irish Party held the balance of power between Conservatives and Liberals. Teaming with the Liberals, the party made its first move, to abolish the veto power of the House of Lords, thus setting the stage for the third Home Rule Bill. Arthur Griffith and Sinn Fein adopted a low profile to see what Redmond could accomplish.

The Liberals balked but finally introduced home rule legislation early in 1912. This brought on the traditional reaction of outrage by the Protestant Ulstermen, who climaxed their threats with a Covenant Day, a massive province-wide rally and oath signing, demanding that they remain British. The marches and the signing of a "covenant" were done by hundreds of thousands of Ulstermen, many affixing their signatures in their own blood. This activity was followed up in 1913 by formation of the Ulster Volunteer Force, a quasi-legal army. When ordered north to break up the activity of the Volunteers, the British Army refused, its officers threatening mutiny before it would fight Protestants. It confirmed what had been known for centuries, that justice for Irish Catholics was a one-way street.

Later in 1913, the same Eoin MacNeill who had co-founded the Gaelic League founded an Irish Volunteer Force for the defense of Irish freedom. The British Army did not look upon this group so benevolently. Meanwhile, funds from Irish-American Fenian groups countered the massive arms shipments to Protestants from Germany.

The Third Home Rule Bill came to a head in 1914, with Protestant Ulster unwilling to budge. Legislation was finally passed that contained a provision preventing the law from going into effect until a future amendment should be added to define county options. By the outset of World War I, what John Redmond had obtained after four years was a bill still years away from becoming law, and providing for possible amendments that would partition the country.

The Irish had again been lied to and cheated. Nonetheless Redmond took England's war cause to the people and some two hundred thousand Irish volunteered for the British forces.

As the war raged on the Continent, an accommodating merchant-Ascendancy element scoffed at the Republicans, and the ordinary people were divided, what with so many of their own in the trenches in France.

Yet Republican yearnings simmered to an inevitable boil, the ranks of Republicans now filled with a roll of future immortals. In 1915 the body of Jeremiah O'Donovan Rossa, the unrepentant Fenian, was returned to Ireland for burial after he had undergone the hells of British prisons and exile in America. The occasion was seized upon to lay him in state, and with a full complement of Irish Volunteers a martyr's funeral was held.

Padraic Pearse, poet, schoolmaster, and high-ranking member of the Brotherhood, as well as leader of the Volunteers, intoned an impassioned eulogy:

". . . we pledge to Ireland our love, and we pledge to English rule in Ireland our hate . . . life springs from death: and from the graves of patriot men and women spring living nations. . . . The Defenders of this Realm . . . think that they have pacified Ireland . . . the fools, the fools, the fools! They have left us our Fenian dead, and while Ireland holds these graves, Ireland unfree shall never be at peace."

The Republicans knew that when the war was done England would turn a massive army on them. With little hope of success, undermanned and underarmed, they knew the time was not good but the future would be no better.

On Easter Monday, 1916, a terrible beauty was born.

THOOR BALLYLEE *A Norman keep used as a summer home by Yeats, co-founder of the National Theater, leader of the literary revival, elected to the Free State Senate, recipient of the Nobel Prize in Literature. But overall, he was the high priest of the nationalistic poets, who never stopped being awed that the power of his words should have inspired Irishmen to rebel.*

The General Post Office, O'Connell Street, Dublin

EASTER MONDAY—1916

For several months there had been a split in the command of the Volunteers. Founder and Chief of Staff Eoin MacNeill was of a notion not to commit the forces unless the British tried to disarm them or attempted to conscript Irishmen into the British Army. The militant element consisted of members of the secret Brotherhood led by Padraic Pearse, the most mystic of poets, and James Connolly, leader of the Irish labor movement.

For a moment, MacNeill was persuaded to go along with the planned insurrection but saw the final madness of it when a German freighter, disguised as a Norwegian, was caught by the British naval patrol and scuttled itself with twenty thousand rifles destined for the Volunteers. Roger Casement, who had negotiated the deal with the German high command, had been captured.

With orders out for nationwide Volunteer "maneuvers" on Easter Monday, MacNeill issued a countermanding directive, which was published in newspapers across Ireland.

Liberty Hall, Dublin, headquarters for the labor movement and a small, militant Citizens' Army, was to be the assembly point for the four Volunteer battalions. The banner across the building read: WE SERVE NEITHER KING OR KAISER BUT IRELAND. They drifted in by foot and bicycle in green uniform of the Citizens' Army and in pale heather of the Volunteers. Some wore only armbands. Because of the confusion in orders only half, some fifteen hundred men, showed, and only half of these were armed. The ranks were laced with members of the Irish Republican Brotherhood.

It was a leisurely day, a bank holiday, and people in the streets paid scant attention as the units deployed. Marches and mock battles were now an everyday occurrence.

147

A series of classic foul-ups, the specialty of Irish rebellions, ensued. One group attacked the Magazine Fort in Phoenix Park containing the ammunition dump but blew up the wrong building, causing scant damage. A second unit entered Dublin Castle unopposed but withdrew to a biscuit factory nearby, thus failing to exploit what would have made an enormous psychological impact.

Other units deployed to strategic locations about the city. Countess Markiewicz took the College of Surgeons on College Green, Edward Daly seized the Four Courts, filled with army records, and Eamon de Valera commanded five undermanned companies at Boland's Flour Mill which bisected a key route from the port to the south into the city.

James Connolly and Padraic Pearse, fully aware they were engaged in a suicide mission, marched up the main street with a column of a hundred and fifty men, halted before the General Post Office, rushed in, seized it, and barricaded themselves. After some confusion, they sent back to Liberty Hall for a flag which arrived in a brown paper bag. The green with the golden harp and the words in Gaelic, The Irish Republic, flew from the pediment and later a second flag, a new concoction, a tricolor of green, white, and orange, flew beside it.

Padraic Pearse went outside and read a proclamation to a mystified and somewhat indifferent crowd of onlookers.

"IRISHMEN AND IRISHWOMEN: In the name of God and of the dead generations from which she receives her old tradition of nationhood, Ireland, through us, summons her children to her flag and strikes for her freedom. . . .

"We declare the right of the people of Ireland to the ownership of Ireland. . . ."

The Citizens' Army, the Volunteers, and the Brotherhood now united and became the Irish Republican Army with Padraic Pearse named President of the "Provisional Government."

A detachment of British Lancers assembled in the street called Sackville by the British and O'Connell by the Irish. They galloped brazenly toward Nelson's Column opposite the GPO. A fusillade from rebel headquarters at the GPO sent them packing into a Gilbert and Sullivan retreat except for that horse that seems to fall dead in every battle.

Later in the day the Liberties, the most obscene ghetto in Europe, erupted onto O'Connell Street and engaged in massive looting before a rebel force under Sean T. O'Kelly, another future President of Ireland, drove them off.

As evening came Irish Fusiliers and Irish Rifles of the British Army were maneuvering into position against rebel headquarters.

By midnight the vast main room of the post office was lit eerily in candlelight. Padraic Pearse went up to the roof and gazed onto the smoldering city as the clocks tolled the hour. He was a man now face to face with his own impending death and filled with mad wonderment at what he had wrought . . . unaware of the pickets around him . . . an ancient Celt returned to frightful destiny.

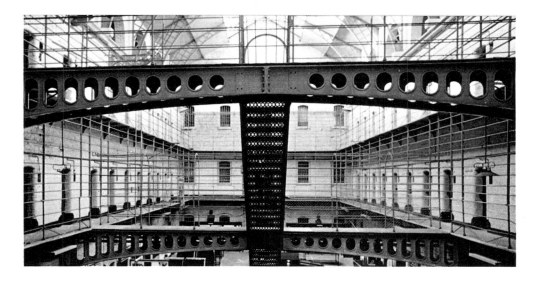

KILMAINHAM JAIL—Dublin

Support risings around the country failed to materialize. The rebels withstood brutal artillery fire until they ran out of food and ammunition. With central Dublin severely shelled and hundreds of casualties drawn on both sides, Pearse issued a surrender order a week after the rising.

All first-rate castles and prisons have ghosts rankling about their corridors but none has so distinguished a list as Kilmainham. Dublin Castle had become wary of the waves created by the French Revolution and decided to increase its own penal capacity should the troublesome Irish stir up.

Kilmainham was opened in 1796, none too soon to receive the United Irishmen of the 1798 Rising, among their numbers Napper Tandy, Samuel Neilson, Henry Joy McCracken, and Theobald Wolfe Tone himself.

Next followed the equally illustrious Robert Emmet, whose rousing speech from the dock was to become a textbook declamation for young patriots. "When my country takes her place among the nations of the earth," he said in 1803 prior to his hanging, "then, and not till then, shall my epitaph be written."

During the famine years William Smith O'Brien, leader of the Young Irelanders who rose in 1848, was to become the next distinguished guest of the Crown.

The procession continued on with the Fenians, poet John O'Leary and the venerable Jeremiah O'Donovan Rossa.

Michael Davitt of the Land League was interned in Kilmainham as was Charles Stewart Parnell. Indeed, a veritable Who's Who of Irish immortals have sanctified that awful place.

The Invincibles Yard was named after the hanging courtyard of a short-lived group who carried out the political assassination of the English chief secretary and under-secretary in 1882 in Phoenix Park.

Cells, therefore, had long awaited the perpetrators of the Easter Rising. The leaders were given a quick secret court-martial and remanded to Kilmainham for execution. Beginning Wednesday, May 3, and continuing through Friday, May 13, they were shot at a rate of one to four a day in Stonebreaker's Yard. Nearly all of them were scholars with early education by the Christian Brothers, Sons of Fenians, some musicians, some poets, and scarcely a military man among them. They met their end without regret, each making a last outcry of defiance, gently or angered. The last to be executed was James Connolly, who had been wounded at the GPO and had to be carried out and placed against the wall tied to a chair.

Roger Casement was hanged in England on August 3. Ninety-seven other death sentences, including those of Countess Markiewicz and Eamon de Valera, were commuted. The Countess was ultimately set free and de Valera given a twenty-year term.

By these sixteen executions the British had accomplished what the rebellion itself had failed to do, and that was to arouse a lethargic Irish people into a rage that would ultimately lead to nationhood.

Padraic Pearse said of himself, Tom MacDonagh, and Joseph Plunkett at the beginning of the rising, "If we do nothing else we shall rid Ireland of three bad poets."

It seems that the British might have learned something about the Irish after all their experience. It is one thing to kill enemy soldiers in battle but one just doesn't go around shooting poets.

A MOST REMARKABLE FAMILY

John MacBride arrived on the Dublin scene from his native Westport in the mid-1890s, treading the classical route of dissenters. The Irish Republican Brotherhood, an old Fenians debating society, lay fallow. Parnell's death had put the damper on so much hope. These were still the moments before the great revivals. MacBride moved on to the Transvaal in Africa.

Earlier, in the Celtic Literary Society, he had met Arthur Griffith, an aspiring journalist, and induced Griffith to join him in the Transvaal. After working as a newsman and for a gold mining company Griffith returned to Dublin filled with MacBride's no-nonsense Fenianism and started up a paper, *The United Irishman*.

In 1899 the Boer War erupted against the British. An Irish brigade, mostly Americans of Irish origin, formed up for the Boers. MacBride went from second to first in command, acquitting himself well in battle and fulfilling the craving to take up arms against the British.

Those pesky Boers ultimately forced the British to call in a half million troops from all parts of the Empire, including Irish units. It was an old replay of Irish fighting each other for and against England and making truth of the adage that these great soldiers did most of their combat in other uniforms. Even though the Irish-British units drew casualties in the thousands the Boers remained in favor in much of Ireland, as well as liberal England. MacBride's brigade consisted of a handful of men, yet so long as they were battling England it caught the imagination of the people. A Transvaal Committee office opened in Dublin in the Celtic Literary Society. The chairwoman was Maud Gonne, as incredible a lady as ever took up the Irish cause.

Born an English Protestant with a father of Irish Ascendancy heritage, she first saw Dublin at the age of sixteen where her widower father served in the military.

Even at this early time she bore on a lithe six-foot frame the regal carriage that stamped her as an uncommon beauty. Her father's death and her own subsequent illness took her to France for recuperation where she met Lucien Millevoye, a French politician-journalist dedicated to France's cause in Alsace-Lorraine. Maud by now had been bitten by Irish Republicanism and Millevoye encouraged her greatly. In an era when women were smothered, Maud Gonne was a free spirit and as Millevoye's mistress bore him two children, with one daughter surviving.

Her affair was muted with her return to Dublin. Continental culture, heady and physical magnificence, poise, inspiration and tireless energy—all these were Maud Gonne as she plunged into the Fenianism that was.

Asking no easy way, she became a beloved figure in the slums and out in the poverty-riddled West, engaging the landlords in social warfare. Along the way she met William Butler Yeats, who never really got over his love for her. A long-standing proposal of marriage was never accepted by her. There was no time for it in the unending days of lecture tours, fund raising for a spectrum of causes, writing articles, organizing and fighting the underdog's battles. In 1900 she formed the Daughters of Erin, the women's Republican arm. Coincidentally she was a wellspring of inspiration for Yeats, who wrote *Cathleen Ni Houlihan* for her, and her opening performances in a makeshift theater were to become another segment of her legend.

The fates were all in order for a short, star-crossed explosion when John MacBride came home from the wars. In 1900, the year they met, Arthur Griffith formed a patriotic organization, Cumann na nGaedheal, which was to be the forerunner of Sinn Fein. MacBride was elected vice-president. However, his moment of great glory was past and he was badly beaten in an election for Parliament. Dublin Castle, still smarting over the Boer War, deported him.

Against all advice, Maud followed MacBride to Paris and was converted to Catholicism; they were married in 1903. After the birth of Sean in 1904 things went to seed quickly. His light extinguished and drinking heavily, MacBride was unable to bear the role of consort to one of the most electrifying women in Europe. No divorce was possible, and so Maud sued for separation, which he resisted, forcing a public airing of dirty laundry. The inner councils of the movement didn't like the tarnishing of an idol and, Irish Catholicism being Irish Catholicism, she was forced to remain in exile when she tried to return home in 1905.

Now the pale ghost of himself, Major John blustered Republicanism from diminished platforms while she stayed in Paris raising her two children.

Faithful to the cause to the end, John MacBride was in Jacob's Biscuit Factory during the Easter Rising, a mere second in command to Thomas MacDonagh. There seemed no real reason to execute MacBride except that the British still remembered the Boer War. At Stonebreaker's Wall he made a last lovely defiance when offered a blindfold. "It's not the first time I've looked down their guns, Father," he told the attending priest.

Maud Gonne MacBride never stopped working for Ireland, starting an important Republican magazine in exile. In 1917 she returned on a fake passport supplied by Yeats. Her final rejection of marriage freed him at last for his own marriage.

The Cell of Major John MacBride—Kilmainham Jail

Maud Gonne MacBride

Sean MacBride, Nobel Peace Laureate

Maud was arrested and imprisoned in 1918 and again in 1922, when she was interned in Kilmainham Jail. After twenty days on a hunger strike the British let her go.

Her son, Sean MacBride, was just eighteen when he accompanied Michael Collins to London, serving as a messenger with the Irish delegation during the Treaty negotiations. As an Anti-Treaty Republican he rose in the ranks of the IRA up to Chief of Staff in the 1930s, finally resigning on the issue of violence. He learned law, preparing a number of brilliant briefs for barristers in the defense of IRA prisoners, and was called to the bar in 1938.

In 1944 he formed a new political party, Clann na Pob-lachta, and in a coalition government was named Foreign Minister in 1948. It was the most progressive Irish government of its era and the one that finally cut the strings with Britain.

Sean MacBride has gone on to become Ireland's most illustrious world champion of human rights. Unexpected but utterly deserved recognition came in 1974 when he was awarded the Nobel Peace Prize.

Founding father and director of Amnesty International, the world organization for the protection of political prisoners, he participates in an unparalleled number of humanitarian activities and closes the circle of a most remarkable family.

PRELUDE TO DISASTER

Redmond's Irish Party reeked of the home rule charade and was blasted from power in the election of 1918 despite the fact that many of the winning Sinn Fein candidates were in prison. In their sweep Sinn Fein had vowed not to take their seats in Westminster, to resist conscription, and to declare a Republic. British prisons bulged with Republicans. but with the anger of the people rising, prisoners were released in an attempted pacification. However, leaders like de Valera and Countess Markiewicz seemed to go out of one prison gate only to enter another.

Early in 1919 the first Dail in Dublin declared independence and named de Valera President. Michael Collins had emerged as the giant of the military people and together with Cathal Brugha took over the expanding Volunteers, who were now officially the IRA.

Britain then proceeded to engulf Ireland in a holocaust. Fifty thousand troops of the Regular Army units, auxiliaries, and the hated Black and Tan mercenaries poured in to augment the Royal Irish Constabulary. Massive jailings begat executions. Villages were burned to the ground and civilian hostages held. Irish industry was systematically destroyed. In Cork, men like MacCurtain were murdered and men like MacSwiney starved in protest in British prisons. Central Cork itself was razed in an act of vengeance. Secret service informers venomized the people.

The Irish battled back with urban terror and assassinations of traitor and British alike. In the countryside, no-quarter guerrilla warfare pitted the small flying columns against outsized British might.

Old colonizers die hard and their "damn the natives, show them the whip" mentality spewed from martial-law generals. It seems that old revolutionaries die even harder and all the king's men could not break the Irish will. In mid-1921 the British Prime Minister, David Lloyd George, called for truce and negotiations.

On meeting the Irish delegation in London, Lloyd George, a Welshman, referred to "we Celts" and then commenced to fleece them at the bargaining table. Ulster continued the demand for partition. In any event, the Irish were out of their element with that crowd in "diplomatic" negotiations.

What Michael Collins and Arthur Griffith were finally coerced into agreeing to after months of conferences was a partitioned country, withdrawal of the status of "Republic" for that of "Free State" dominion, loyalty to the Crown, British bases and garrisons on her soil, a limitation on her own army, and a variety of debts to Britain.

The Treaty split Sinn Fein and the IRA down the middle, but under an ultimatum by Lloyd George to accept or to face destruction, the Dail passed it by a two-vote majority. The Republic was again rescinded and de Valera resigned.

On that awful night in London when Michael Collins agreed to the Treaty he was to prophesy his own end in a letter to a friend:

"When you have sweated, toiled, had mad dreams, and hopeless nightmares you find yourself in London's streets, cold and dank in the night air. Think—what have I got for Ireland? Something which she has wanted these past seven-hundred years? Will anyone be satisfied at the bargain? Will anyone? I tell you this—early this morning I signed my death warrant."

GENERAL TOM AND LESLIE BARRY *Commandant of the Third Cork and later Chief of Staff of the IRA, Tom Barry was the most brilliant and beloved of the field generals. His West Cork flying columns made hell on earth for the Black and Tans. A genius at welding and inspiring men and a fearless fighter, General Tom is a living legend.*

Leslie, a Dubliner, was in the GPO during the Easter Rising as a nurse and messenger, slipping in and out disguised as a schoolgirl from a nearby convent. For years she was president of the Irish Red Cross.

BEALNABLATH—COUNTY CORK *A few miles from his birthplace, a monument marks the spot where "The Big Fellow" Michael Collins was ambushed and killed in 1922 in the Civil War which followed the Treaty. He was thirty-two.*

JOE CLARKE *was in an outpost of de Valera's command during the Easter Rising. When they became enemies later, the unrepentant Republican in his late nineties made good his vow to outlive Dev.*

MARTIN McGUINNESS *commanded the IRA Brigade in the Bogside of Free Derry at the age of twenty-two. His tiny force destroyed a good part of the city and tied up thousands of British troops and armor. Now "life on the run" has given him a growing intimacy with prisons. His aim remains uncluttered— a united country and a decent job.*

THE IRA

The rejection of the Treaty split party, army, family, and nation. Eamon de Valera led the Republican faction while the Pro-Treaty Free Staters aligned behind Michael Collins and Arthur Griffith.

It started as a queer war, with both sides feeling each other out and operating openly in the cities. The Republicans seized the Four Courts. As the carnage of Civil War commenced, it began to take on shades of the fight against the British, with Free Staters the cumbersome force holding the garrisons while the Republicans used the old tactics of the flying column. Infighting in the urban areas was particularly vicious.

The British heavily backed the Free Staters to ensure their continued presence in a dominion loyal to the Crown. British arms poured in to the Pro-Treaty forces, and British soldiers padded their ranks. With the Free State in control of the civil machinery, finances, and propaganda, and with a preponderance of arms, they launched fratricide on their fellow Irish. Brutal interrogations, secret trials, and executions were inhumane and manifest. When the Republicans were forced to spike their guns in 1924, some twelve thousand, including hundreds of women, were left to rot in prison. A pall of bitter-

ness hung over them that would survive the ages.

De Valera was the last prisoner of Kilmainham. Although the Republicans won a number of seats in the Free State Dail, they refused to enter, for they would neither take an oath to the King nor recognize the Free State and the demise of the Republic.

Final acts of treachery were played by the British when Eoin MacNeill headed a delegation to England to adjust the boundaries imposed in 1922 between the Free State and Northern Ireland. The arbitrary and ridiculous border has been described as a drunk reeling through a dark room. Having snatched off six counties for the "new" Ulster, the Unionists refused to budge and MacNeill ultimately resigned from the commission in disgust. Finally Winston Churchill extracted an agreement to a massive debt that the Free State "owed" England and that squeezed out the last ounce of Irish blood. What England had left was a ravaged land, an impoverished and divided people, a partitioned province with a few crumbs of self-determination, and the seeds of continuing conflict.

From then on the IRA has existed as a sub rosa, semi-legal shadow force still claiming its authority from the abandoned Republic and dedicated to reuniting Ireland through a continued repudiation of the Treaty.

De Valera formed a new party and returned to power, at first tolerating his old Republican comrades but enlisting top IRA people into the police and military, for it was good business to have them keep an eye on the remnants of the movement.

In the early 1930s the IRA was briefly needed. An anti-Communist wave swept Europe, often taking form in fascist street gangs. The fever reached Ireland through an ultra-right-wing organization called the Blueshirts. The IRA met them head on in the street fighting. It boiled to a head when the Blueshirts threatened a march on Dublin that smelled like a coup. Dormant IRA men by the thousands poured into the capital for a showdown, and at the last moment the Blueshirts wisely called off the march.

By the eve of World War II the IRA was again flirting with the Germans for money and arms and launched an ill-advised bomb campaign against England which enraged public opinion there. De Valera was determined to keep Ireland neutral. His dilemma worsened when the IRA pulled off a dazzling raid against the Magazine Fort in Phoenix Park, stripping the bulk of the Irish Army's reserve of guns and ammunition.

It was not so easy to get convictions against IRA men, for Republicanism was deep-seated and an alter ego for the masses. This condition, along with IRA jury tampering, brought on legislation that suspended civil liberties and resulted in intern-

SEAN MacSTIOFAIN *An English-born former Chief of Staff of fanatical intensity, Sean MacStiofain exercised authoritarian control over the IRA and was the architect of the recent bomb campaign. Imprisoned in the Republic, he aborted the hunger strike that would have brought martyrdom. Automatically relieved of his command, he has faded into the background.*

MARIE DRUMM *is a Belfast housewife, grandmother, supermarket manager, and vice president of Sinn Fein. Her oldest son interned, her husband has spent more time in jail than any living Republican and she herself has been imprisoned on both sides of the border. The issues are plain, and her leadership is practiced at the head of the march.*

155

ments without charges that reeked of totalitarianism. The ranks of the IRA were ruthlessly decimated. The horrors of imprisonment became legendary. One IRA staff man was thrown into solitary for three years with only a single blanket for clothing, and for seven years he was not allowed a single letter or visitor. The IRA kept up hunger strikes, riots, and daring escapes but by 1941 the movement had hit rock bottom.

It muddled through the fifties and early sixties in back rooms off back alleys. The powerful American support organizations had long gone.

After fifty years of Protestant abuses in Ulster and the most corrupt political establishment of any British domain, the Catholics were compelled to form Civil Rights protests. These were met by mob action at the goading of demagogues and police thuggery and followed up by British Army brutality and a suspension of both civil and human rights.

IRA units sprang up in the Catholic ghettos of Belfast and Derry that first defended the ghettos and later met savagery head on with violence and counterviolence that now mutilates that tortured place. History will pass on the rights and wrongs, but it was the reborn IRA that forced the issues and a dramatic turnaround in British thinking.

No guerrilla force can function without the support of its own population, and no Catholic in Belfast will ever again throw himself on the tender mercy of the Royal Ulster Constabulary or the British Army. The IRA came back into being at the end of the sixties because of recent decades and past centuries of degradation of the Catholics.

Political impotence continues to be the bane of the IRA. They will not sit down and negotiate because they haven't forgotten, nor will they ever again trust the British and what "we Celts" did to Michael Collins. They are without propaganda machinery to counter the constant reviling of the British, and their lack of political policy and their blind stubbornness have been self-defeating. The British announce weekly that the IRA is dead or badly wounded, but they don't understand that only men die, ideas never die, and the IRA is not an army but an idea. Other revolutionary forces have faded away or taken part in society as loyal opposition. The IRA will do likewise when the Irish case is closed with justice and not till then.

Ireland is a land of storytellers, with IRA tales rating right up there with those of the Celts—a source of amusement at their wild capers and of pride in their martyred heroes. It is a swing back at repression. It is something over which to shed great tears at the Abbey and to sing songs about in the pub of a dark winter's night.

It is the black sheep son, that star-touched dreamer and poet with a heart of the courage of Finn MacCool. It is, all told, the unbeaten fighting spirit of the Irish people themselves.

IN THE STEPS OF MAEVE

Mother of all fighting Irishwomen is Maeve, Queen of Connaught and a central figure of the Celtic epic, *The Cattle Raid of Cooley*.

Although not overly recognized in the pages of history, Irishwomen have been there with pike and pitchfork, gaining full prominence in the Easter Rising and its aftermath and achieving feared and sobering status in today's events.

It is doubtful if anyone was ever less likely a candidate for the role of Irish revolutionary than Constance Gore-Booth, a London-born heiress of an Anglo-Irish Ascendancy landholding family. Her early life was a pampered romp about the estates in Sligo and an arty stint in Paris. Bit by bit she built a backlog of social conscience, and then the foundation of Gaelicism was set when she met Yeats.

After marriage to the Polish Count Markiewicz she moved with him to a Dublin of 1903 throbbing with the excitement of the revival. She plunged fully into the cause of the poor and the cause of Irish freedom. By 1915, when the Irish Volunteers were formed, she was the Maeve among them.

In the Easter Rising, the Countess Markiewicz, wearing a skirted green uniform and toting a now enshrined long stock pistol, was second in command to Michael Mallin at St. Stephen's Green.

After capture and internment at Kilmainham she was transferred to Mountjoy Prison, her life being spared, and finally to Aylesbury in England. She was converted to Catholicism before her release in 1917. Her activities put her back into Holloway Jail in London. As a prisoner of that place she won an election as Sinn Fein candidate from a district of Dublin, becoming the first woman ever elected to Westminster. It was a seat she never took.

Named by the Second Dail as Secretary of Labor, she underwent her next prison term in Cork, where she paid the jail the knowledgeable compliment of being the most comfortable of them all.

Constance Markiewicz, jailed again in 1920, fought after her release with the Anti-Treaty forces in the Civil War, living "on the run" with men half her age. Her final defiance was a hunger strike in 1923.

This remarkable woman died weary in 1927. Her daughter's name was Maeve.

OUGHTERARD—Easter Sunday

This year, next year. It will be pretty much the same. The doors of the village church open and the people of the town scurry to protect their finest from the downpour. The courtyard boasts the new affluence . . . a full lot of automobiles.

The local IRA unit forms up, and one of them calls over a bullhorn exhorting everyone not to forget the memorial service. There aren't many takers. The troubles up North seem remote enough and sometimes they wish to hell these people would stop remembering.

A handful of the faithful trudge behind the pipers down the main road out of town, the rear brought up by three local constables.

The Irish tricolor flutters feebly in the soggy chill. Some of the new generation have taken the oath. They may well live as outlaws in their own land. Despite the thin disguise of dark glasses, everyone knows who they are, but they are safe unless another periodic purge shuts them away in prison.

At the site of the common plot the annual Easter Proclamation of the IRA is read. The message is always the same. There will be no peace until the six counties of Ulster are reunited with the rest of Ireland. Then a bent old man steps forward and recites the prayers in Gaelic.

They've had their kicking around all right. So many of their

own have no use for them. There was a time during the Civil War when they were refused the sacraments of the Church. Why, old Tom Barry out of Cork was excommunicated four times.

During all the internments they refused to recognize the authority of the courts or even to wear prison uniforms, standing on the principle that they were political prisoners. No amount of brutality or persecution did them in.

Up North they are characterized as hoodlums, killers, and gunmen. The old anti-Irish bromides. There is nothing unique about it. Few revolutionaries of any age have won the endearment of the ruling class.

In Scotland and Wales the wasted men of those English principalities are faced with the dual choice of emigrating or taking to the bottle.

In Ireland, there is a third choice.

Over in a corner there is a lone drinker. A man down from the North. He doesn't say much. Everyone, including the local garda, knows who he is. He's got a lot on his mind. He's about to slip back over the border into Newry.

There's a wife and five kids . . . hasn't been able to find work for three years. His father before him went without a job for the last twenty years of his life.

There's a lot to remember. When he was a kid in Derry there was that Orange Parade on Apprentice Boys Day passing over the Bogside ghetto. They were beating the Lambeg drums so hard their hands bled, and they showered pennies down on him and his people, shouting obscenities to the Pope. Some stone throwing started and the parade turned into a pogrom. The Royal Ulster Constabulary stood by as the ghetto was burned.

His auld man was killed that day.

He is a nameless fighter of the IRA.

DEV

The son of Kate Coll, an Irish immigrant domestic, and Vivion de Valera, a Spanish music teacher, Eamon de Valera was born in Brooklyn in 1882. His father died a few years after his birth and he was sent to Ireland to be raised by relatives in a rather sad, rather lonely boyhood. Skimping through school on an Irish shoestring, he dallied with the idea of priesthood but abandoned it for a mathematics degree, which brought him to Dublin as a teacher.

Dev joined the Gaelic League more for culture than revolution and learned the Irish language from Sinead Flanagan, whom he married in 1908.

Two years later he was signed on as a lecturer at Maynooth, solidifying that kind of devotion to Catholicism that would take him to his private chapel for prayer any number of times a day. His thinking was always tuned to include the position of the Hierarchy. When de Valera joined the Volunteers at its founding in 1913, he was far removed from Connolly's socialism and Pearse's Celtic mysticism. Although a top commander, he never joined their inner councils. De Valera was a pragmatist and with the cool detachment of a mathematics teacher he studied the area he knew he would command in the Easter Rising. He fought extremely well, surrendering only at the command of his superiors.

A quirk of fate saved him from the firing squad. His half brother in America, a priest, appealed to the President, who intervened to save his life.

The rest of that turbulent era saw Dev rise in the political arena and depart from the Brotherhood. As one of the leaders of the proclaimed but unrecognized Republic he was jailed in England, where Michael Collins engineered an ingenious escape for him. He fled to America, raising funds and attempting to get recognition for the Republic.

Leading the Anti-Treaty forces in the Civil War, he lived on the run, and surrender once again took him to prison. The shattered remnants of Sinn Fein were still strong enough to win fifty-seven seats in the Dail in the election of 1925. Nonetheless there was the question of an oath they would not take.

In 1926, de Valera formed the Fianna Fail Party, which was to be the dominating force in Irish politics for the coming decades. Drinking from a bitter cup, de Valera took the oath in order to seat his party. He knew he lied when he took it and so did everyone else. Some called this act traitorous, but in reality there was no other route to political power. By 1932 Fianna Fail was within a hairbreadth of being the majority party and was able, by a coalition with seven Labor seats, to form a government.

During all this, Sinead was to raise a family of eight children, remaining an uncomplaining, saintly woman in the background. De Valera was beset by his own malady, pending blindness. A half dozen operations were ultimately unable to stave off almost total loss of sight.

He went about the business of divorcing Ireland from Britain. It had to be done piecemeal. The rescinding of the hated oath was followed by a new constitution and a long and bitter war with England over payment of annuities and tariffs. The battle climaxed when Britain gave up rights to the Treaty ports on the eve of World War II.

De Valera was obsessed with keeping Ireland neutral, the epic question of his regime. She had no quarrel, no reason to go to war, particularly England's war. On the other hand she isolated herself even further, stunted her own progress, and cast aspersions on her own morality as a Western democracy.

De Valera had become head of a badly mauled little nation, divided within, taking its first floundering free steps. The era required a strong hand. He earned a full complement of enemies in the process.

There were gaping flaws in his government, as well there would be for any national leader of such long tenure. De Valera never succeeded in reunification or in pacifying the IRA. His suppression of the IRA was every bit as severe as the British behavior. Despite cutting the ties with England, he was not the man who finally proclaimed the Republic.

He never had the fine grasp of an Irish relationship with the world, nor did he bring economic fulfillment. Dr. Charles McQuaid, the most reactionary churchman of his day, and his ilk always seemed to have his ear, veering him away from true social progress.

There was, moreover, a bit of something in the man that seemed to want to keep Ireland a pastoral, Gaelic-speaking, semi-monastic, aloof cultural jewel. It was a queer two-edged sword, with a flair for world statesmanship in one blade and isolationism in the other.

It is to be remembered he dominated the Irish scene for over a half century—twice President of the early "Republics," Prime Minister in two separate stretches. The first ran a decade and a half, and the second, nearly a decade. Finally, in 1959 he began to serve another two terms as President before retirement in 1973.

Eamon de Valera had the full measure of that detached, ruthless arrogance, political guile, persuasiveness, and total self-assurance that stamp greatness on a national leader. He was of the rarest breed, the head of a small country that has achieved stature among the political giants of this century.

Book Two

ULSTER

1. THE RED HAND OF ULSTER
—Plantation and Genesis of Conflict

Queen Mary, the original Bloody Mary, first conjured up the notion of plantations. She was the Catholic daughter of Henry VIII, her reign sandwiched between her father's and Elizabeth's. Although she was a Roman Catholic, it should be noted in fairness that she treated Catholics with the same mistrust and hatred as she did Protestants.

Counties Offaly and Leix were purged of the O'Mores and O'Connors, whose lands were confiscated and who were sent packing to be replaced by an importation of English farmers. The plantation did not take hold. Likewise a later plantation syndicate in Munster headed by Sir Walter Raleigh collapsed in a Fitzgerald rising.

Ulster was the plantation that came to stay. Although the great O'Neill Clan paid titular homage to the Crown, Ulster was still largely ruled by the ancient Celtic Brehon code of tribal and religious law. Of all the rebellious elements, the O'Neills remained most constant, forcing Elizabeth's generals into a succession of battles. After the defeat at Kinsale in 1602 and the "Flight of the Earls" in 1607 the bite was put on to neutralize the O'Neills and their allies forever.

James I, Elizabeth's successor, moved to plant Ulster at just about the same time that he planted the colony of Virginia to deal with the "Indian problem." A hundred and fifty thousand Scots were imported to accomplish the feat. O'Neill lands were dissected and snatched up at fourpence an acre; a few hundred pounds bought a borough, and a thousand pounds bought a barony and the title to go with it. Derry was granted to the guilds of London, and fortress towns were erected against the avenging wrath of the savage natives. Preachermen were also planted, but the language barrier and no love for Britain left them no more successful than the conversion attempts during the Reformation.

Owen Roe O'Neill returned from the Continent to participate in a rage of warfare that commenced with a Catholic peasant rising in 1641 marked by the massacre of Presbyterians. This was avenged in full measure under Cromwell by a far broader set of murders and the confiscation of what was left of any decent land.

In 1685, James II, the last Catholic monarch of England, ascended the throne, causing an immediate parliamentary crisis but renewing hope in Ireland that the plantation would be abolished. As James alienated both Whig and Tory at home, he openly wooed the Catholics of Ireland, a perfectly natural ally. Fearing James's bold strokes and a renewal of Catholic succession to the throne, his opposition came up with William of Orange, a Dutchman, who landed in England in 1688 with the overwhelming support of the establishment.

James fled, first seeking support from France and then going to Ireland to set up his forces. Although he promised religious toleration and no confiscation of lands held by Presbyterians, his presence reminded them well of the massacres of 1641 and they fled into the fortified cities.

After obtaining allegiance in the south his forces moved to Ulster, set siege to Londonderry, and unsuccessfully bid to capture Enniskillen. William's troops under his Dutch generals soon followed to Ulster, and the epic confrontation took place at the Boyne River on July 1, 1690. James was beaten. Shortly thereafter a treaty was signed at Limerick securing the Protestant stranglehold. James's army was allowed to enter France. Some fifteen thousand of Ireland's best fighting men went into an exile known as the "Flight of the Wild Geese."

The bitter fruits of defeat were Penal Laws aimed at the

destruction of the Irish Catholics as a human breed. Edmund Burke noted that "the penal code was a machine of as wise and elaborate contrivance for the impoverishment and degradation of the people, and the debasement of them, of human nature itself, as ever proceeded from the perverted ingenuity of man."

As non-Anglicans, Scottish Presbyterians were also deemed inferior and were to come under some aspects of the penal code. However, there existed an "Ulster tradition" of protecting certain basic rights of Presbyterian farmers that spared them from the full fate of the Catholics. Nonetheless, the heavy hand of the Ascendancy and gentry weighed tellingly and brought on an emigration of some two hundred thousand Scots to America during the eighteenth century. These were the Scotch-Irish, a remarkable caliber of pioneers of a sternly devout and industrious ilk. As frontiersmen they dealt with the Indians as they had dealt with the Catholics in taking and holding their land. As fighters they were in the top rank of the American Revolution. American Presidents of Scotch-Irish background count Andrew Jackson, Polk, Buchanan, Andrew Johnson, Grant, Arthur, Cleveland, Harrison, McKinley, and Wilson.

The penal code decayed under pressure of the new Irish nationalists, members of the Protestant Ascendancy who wanted Ireland as their own country and who cried out for their repressed brothers. Inspired by the French Revolution, the Irish Parliament grew bold in its legislation, no longer the automatic servant of the Crown. Outside parliamentary confines, the United Irishmen, also of Ascendancy stock, geared for their own armed rising.

While this developed among the intelligentsia, a vicious round of agrarian warfare shaped up in the countryside. As land-starved Catholic peasants gained the right to bid on leases, they often undercut the more conservative and long-established Presbyterians. Night riding and raids by opposing gangs grew bloody and sectarian in character. The Presbyterians had been

fellow sufferers in the beginning. They had brought from Scotland a tradition of liberalism. However, by the time of the United Irish Uprising in 1798 they were dead set against the Catholics on religious lines. Presbyterians in the Yeomanry were particularly brutal in suppressing the rising. The formation of the Orange Order out of the Presbyterian raiders and the Yeomanry gave formal expression to Catholic hating and opened a gaping wound that remains unhealed.

Britain was now faced with a recently suppressed but not forgotten rising, for the seeds of nationalism were sown. She was further faced with a mounting drive for Catholic emancipation and an Irish Parliament that would no longer serve England. It was time to take Irish matters out of Irish hands and she did so shamefully. Twenty-eight new Irish peers were created, and twenty-six promotions to existing peerages as well as a hundred seats in Commons were held out as bait. The Irish were coerced and bribed into dissolving their own Parliament. The Act of Union in 1800 was to add the cross of St. Patrick to the cross of St. George and the Scottish cross of St. Andrew to form the Union Jack, signifying a United Kingdom. Those Irish who went to Lords and Commons were literally powerless as Dublin Castle now ruled unchallenged.

The Act of Union came under fire immediately and remained so for the better part of a century until Parnell was able to muster enough Irish Party strength in Westminster to open the home rule struggle. However, the Act of Union was Protestant Ulster's protection against the "harlot of Rome," and Ulster reacted accordingly. Any threat of a divorcement from Britain by home rule sent them rioting, signing covenants in blood, arming, and threatening—all sung to a tune of obsessive loyalty to the Crown.

From the time of Daniel O'Connell's fight for Catholic emancipation, any Catholic gain was considered by the Protestants a threat against them. Each new reform or relief measure polarized them on religious lines and they, likewise, characterized all Catholics as anti-British nationalists.

The Protestant community as a body was close-minded and bigoted. Fear of Catholicism was real enough, for what the Protestants really feared was that others would do to them what they had done to others. In the same vein, their professed love of the Crown was not so much a love of the Crown as a love of themselves and a need for a big daddy to protect them.

They joined together in odd spectrums of society—the gentry with the ordinary man, people who had nothing in common except preservation of the status quo. Their desire was to remain living in the past.

Out of their experience has come a unique species, the Ulsterman who is not Irish or British. He has a precarious piece of a province and a life in siege and in limbo. His fears have been milked by generations of hate-spewing preachers who have

made Ulster the largest Bible belt per capita in the world, for the Ulsterman must constantly be reminded of his self-righteousness and constantly rededicated to his self-defense, to warding off siege in order to retain control of the paranoid society he has created.

He feels isolated and alone and surrounded by enemies, those from whom he has usurped the land and a decent quality of life. It is his British connection he must have as protection from the conquered majority. The Ulsterman pays his dues by proof of loyalty in spilling inordinate amounts of blood in Britain's wars. His medal, his title, and his rank are his passbook to life and everlasting glory.

From its conception Ulster was established as a fortress outpost of colonial exploitation. These people were put there to replace the natives. The prime reason for their existence in Ulster was to give loyalty.

A principle of this tragic place is the automatic assumption that the native is disloyal and that therefore any form of protest over his degrading status is considered proof of disloyalty.

What happened at the siege of Londonderry and the Battle of the Boyne formed the charter of a culture that smells strangely of Aryan supremacy. The Ulsterman's own sense of godliness and the subhuman character he had created out of the native Irishman allows him to impose and justify any sort of debasement. It is all a pure concept of Nazi ideology.

There is a sick play on Christianity, with Londonderry having gained the stature of a holy city and the Boyne being construed as the most important battle in Christian survival. Part and parcel is the Ulsterman's belief that he is truly waging God's fight and that therefore the other people and their religion must be anti-God. From the mouths and minds of an unbroken succession of hatemongers, the Catholic faith has been portrayed as a satanic clique with James II and the Pope as chief devils and fiends. William of Orange has been distorted out of all reality as a super-Christ. Actually, the Dutchman was a rather decent sort (who, incidentally, had the Pope's backing against James).

Somehow, it's not all that lofty. The Crown and the British gentry have worked a simple game plan, manipulating peasant and worker so as to keep the classes separated and fighting. It is the classic application of divide and rule. The Protestant, particularly the Presbyterian, has been robotized by the use of God, King, and country and whatever fear tactic would work in sponsoring hostility to his neighbor and creating a permanent siege mentality.

Through all the agony a little true Christianity would have gone a long way in solving matters, but one must eventually come to realize that this is an unhealthy land and Ulsterism is the ultimate perversion of Christianity.

171

The ancestral home of Woodrow Wilson nestles on the slopes of the Sperrin Mountains in County Tyrone. William Tom Wilson and his sister Susan, born and raised on the original homestead, are third cousins of the late American President.

The Ulsterman glorifies his province as a noble work of God and man where life is far superior to that of the Republic. In fact, the grass is greener on the Ulster side of the fence. Trappings of affluence are everywhere and would be envied by most countries in Europe and by Britain itself. For a great number of Ulstermen the quality of material life indeed surpasses that of the South.

The Ulsterman is apt to lump his luxuries into a general Aryan thesis extolling his own industriousness. After all, he reasons, the Catholics are largely a feckless, childbearing lot who would rather live on the dole than work.

Lest he forget, the Catholic farms were up in the heather with the rocks. The Ulsterman was granted the best land, privileges, protection, and jobs as payment for his undivided loyalty. Nor was he sacked and pillaged and bled by rents and taxation as was his counterpart in the South.

The main reason for his well-being, however, is that Britain chose to industrialize Ulster while the rest of Ireland was kept as England's cattle ranch.

The Industrial Revolution was late in coming, but when it did it came with the impact of a flash flood. The province has a formidable manufacturing complex that classifies it as a small giant. Built on a base of linen, its textile product has survived the depressed periods to become a staple world commodity, and the behemoth shipyards of Belfast hold the largest drydocks in the British Isles; but so long as jobs are held as ransom, it has only added to Ulster's woes.

Linen factory, Sion Mills, County Tyrone

**THE GIANT'S CAUSEWAY—
COUNTY ANTRIM** *One has the choice
of accepting the geologists' explanation
of this phenomenon as a curious cooling
of a basalt-based volcanic outflow or the
more esoteric rationale that it was the
personal handiwork of that fellow Finn
MacCool building steppingstones to
Scotland.*

*It was near here that the first legend-
ary O'Neill sailed toward Ulster against
other contenders, the first one landing
to claim the kingdom. Within sight of
shore and wanting desperately to win,
the O'Neill cut off his right hand and
flung it on land—thus, the Red Hand of
Ulster.*

THE GLENS OF ANTRIM *There are
nine glens on the Antrim coast, Glenariff
and its lush misty vale being the most
magnificent. This is the heartland of the
Scottish settlement, good land sloping
down to the sea and blessed by a hard-
working, pious, and earthy folk. Scotland remained the main market until a
coastal road was built in 1832. It was
accomplished by dynamiting the cliffs
into the sea to form the roadbed and
was considered one of the great engineering feats of the time.*

174

GLENARIFF *The glens, coast, and rolling hills epitomize Ulster's rare scenic beauty.*

THE BIRTH OF A NATION

Ulstermen paid in blood during World War I to sanctify themselves as loyalists and enhance their position in future negotiations. What was never to be forgotten was that, while the illustrious Ulster regiments hurled themselves into battle at the Somme, those despicable rebels of the Republic were stabbing Britain in the back by a rising at home. (Actually, the British forces contained more volunteers from among the Catholic population, but in large measure the Catholics got traditional second-class treatment.)

The Home Rule Bill was abrogated by a Government of Ireland Act in 1920 which called for a legislative body again to be established in Dublin. There were provisions for a dual commonwealth in the event that Protestant Ireland in the North didn't wish to remain in the Free State.

From the turn of the century the Unionist Party had become the political arm of Protestant Ulster. It was born in an Orange Order hall and its destinies were led by Edward Carson, a Dubliner steeped in the Protestant cause, and James Craig. Craig, who ascended to the leadership, had been a lifelong foursquare servant of the Crown from the Boer War onward with distinguished service in the military, the civil service, and Westminster.

Before the conferences commenced Craig and the Unionists studied their maps intently to determine what they could legitimately claim. At first they wanted all nine counties that made up Ulster but concluded that it would invite a Catholic majority and make the holding of it extremely difficult. With great reluctance Craig conceded that the counties of Cavan, Monaghan, and Donegal, with topheavy Catholic populations, would have to go into the Free State. But even in claiming six counties the Unionists displayed tremendous arrogance, for Catholic majorities existed in many areas.

Moreover, the city of Londonderry historically and economically was tied to Donegal and held a Catholic majority. But it would have been unthinkable in the Orange, Unionist, Protestant mind to create a new state without their holy city, and the Protestants were bound to have it even at the price of amputating it from its natural hinterland.

A truce in the fighting in Ireland brought delegations to London in the summer of 1921. Michael Collins was obviously concerned by the enormity of the Craig and Unionist demands. At this point Lloyd George deliberately deceived him by putting a meaningless clause in the Treaty articles which called for a future commission to adjust boundaries. At the same time the Unionists got what they asked for. The language of the clause clearly stated that boundaries would be readjusted according to the wishes of the majority of the people in each disputed area.

Had Lloyd George been telling the truth, it would have followed that the greater part of Counties Tyrone and Fermanagh and their heavy Catholic majorities, as well as the densely populated Catholic enclaves in Down and Armagh, would go into the Free State. West Londonderry, adjacent to Donegal, unquestionably also belonged in the Free State. Collins clung to this clause as a false hope, although he must have been aware that Lloyd George was leading him down the garden path.

Collins signed the Treaty on December 6, 1921. One day later the Unionists exercised their option to stay out of the Free State and declared Northern Ireland a province of Britain.

In Southern Ireland Pro- and Anti-Treaty forces engaged in a Civil War and at the same time Northern Ireland moved to solidify her newborn state.

There was very little fighting in Northern Ireland during the Civil War except for massive anti-Catholic pogroms. Nonetheless Ulster pulled up the drawbridges, was loaded to the gunwales with British arms, and augmented her newly formed Constabulary with sixty thousand auxiliary troops, entirely Protestant in character. Of the auxiliaries, the B-Specials, a civil militia mostly of Orangemen, were to gain a well-deserved infamy for their brutal tactics.

The announced reason behind the formation of sixty thousand auxiliaries in addition to the Constabulary and British Army was to protect Ulster from IRA "murderers" and "gangsters." This is a tenaciously held fabrication or a stretched half-truth at best. The true purpose was to have a ready instrument of terror and intimidation over the Catholic population, one third of Ulster's people.

From the beginning, no protest ever failed to bring on a reaction of overkill. It was a blunt instrument of totalitarianism. To back up those massive forces, a Special Powers Act was legislated at the very start to enable this one-party government to arrest anyone without warrant or reason and to hold him behind bars indefinitely without charges or rights. It is small wonder this act would become a model law for later fascist regimes in Europe.

The original justification for the Special Powers Act was as an emergency measure during the "troubles," but it was renewed annually until it became permanent law in 1933, and it has remained on the books. It is painfully clear that the Ulsterman considers his very existence as a permanent state of emergency within a perennial siege. Accordingly the B-Specials kept their weapons in their homes. Likewise, tens of thousands of private guns were licensed to individuals under

Sir Edward Carson, co-founder of Northern Ireland, stands before Stormont, Parliament of the besieged province.

the cover and charade of "hunting clubs." Protestant hunting clubs, that is. In one form or another some two hundred thousand men had arms out of a total Protestant population of a million people.

In 1924 the Border Commission commenced work in London. The finality of Lloyd George's treachery crashed down on the Free State. A new Protestant banality was added to the old ones . . . "not an inch." After a futile year Eoin MacNeill resigned in disgust and the extorted borders became reality.

There can be absolutely no doubt of Unionist intentions from the inception of Northern Ireland. In the words of Craig, later Viscount Craigavon, "Ours is a Protestant Government and I am an Orangeman. . . . All I boast of is that we are a Protestant Parliament and a Protestant State."

Sir Basil Brooke, later Lord Brookborough, architect of the auxiliaries and later Prime Minister, was even more to the point. "Many in the audience employ Catholics, but I have not one about my place. Catholics are out to destroy Ulster. . . . Ninety-seven per cent of the Roman Catholics in Northern Ireland are disloyal. . . ."

Had it ever been intended that the Catholics be given a stake in Northern Ireland, it is entirely reasonable to assume that the IRA would have disappeared for lack of need. But when Northern Ireland came into being, one third of her people were earmarked for destitution. Britain had granted Ulster an exalted status far beyond that of a mere province and even beyond that of Scotland and Wales. How a democratic nation allowed this to happen within her own midst defies explanation, and how this monstrous regime managed to pull it off for fifty years reads like something out of *Alice in Wonderland*.

177

2. THE ORANGE ORDER

To the glorious, pious and immortal memory of good King William who saved us from rogues and roguery, slaves and slavery, knaves and knavery, from brass money and wooden shoes: and whoever denies this toast may be slammed, crammed and jammed into the muzzle of the great gun of Athlone, and the gun fired into the Pope's belly, and the Pope into the devil's belly and the devil into hell, and the door locked and the key forever in an Orangeman's pocket.

The sorry part of this traditional toast is that it isn't rendered with tongue in cheek. The tone and mentality are established for one of man's more incredible institutions, one that could only be conceived and prosper in a hate-riddled atmosphere such as Ulster's.

It was the Orange Order, begun in and about County Armagh around 1780. Secret Presbyterian bands rode the nights to intimidate landlords and their agents into keeping rents and conditions bearable.

As the penal codes eroded, Catholic Relief acts were legislated, giving Catholics permission to bid on land tenancies. The night riders were converted into anti-Catholic vigilantes bent on burning them out of Ulster.

The Catholics replied in kind with The Defenders, and for years sectarian agrarian raids swept Armagh and the surrounding counties. A showdown fight occurred in 1795 in a place called the Diamond near Armagh Township in which the Protestant Peep-o'-Day Boys won out over The Defenders. The same night they glorified the victory by renaming their organization after William of Orange, their savior of a century earlier.

Warrants for new Orange Lodges soon numbered over a hundred. At first this was viewed with suspicion by Dublin Castle. The roughneck element, a secret armed force, and continuing excesses were all cause for concern. Yet by the time of the United Irish Rising in 1798 there were an estimated two hundred thousand members. They entered the rising massively on the side of the British in the Yeomanry and militia. In neutralizing Ulster they were able to establish a permanent presence.

Torture, lashings, executions, and burnings by the Yeomanry reached such maniacal proportions that a British commander resigned in disgust. The Orange composition of the Yeomanry was father, forerunner, and example of brutality to be emulated a hundred and twenty-five years later by the B-Specials.

The Orange Order was molded on a pseudo-Masonic structure replete with secret oaths, handshakes, and passwords with an enormity of prayer and a rash of exotic-sounding ranks such as Royal Scarlets, Purple Marksmen, Black Perceptories, Apron and Blue, Link and Chain. The founding principles, quite unchanged, were allegiance to the Crown, upholding the Protestant Ascendancy, and hatred of Catholics.

At first there was a cautious and mixed reaction from the gentry. With the coming of the nineteenth century and the drive for Catholic emancipation, the gentry began to find the Orange Order usable. "Gentlemen's Lodges," largely political in character, sprang up to tangle with the issues. A yearly march and a patronizing pat on the head to the lesser brothers brought these two unlikely ends of the society together in common cause. The grass-roots and universal membership gave the "Gentlemen's Lodges" an outside muscle.

An infusion of preachers in the early 1800s served to give the ordinary lodges a semblance of respectability. The preachers could talk directly to the common man, who essentially had

banded together for self-protection. The Orange pot was always kept stewing with stories that the Pope and his convincing Jesuits were planning night and day to take over Ulster. Always militant and always ready, the Orangemen have proved to be easily incited. Beginning with the Rev. Dr. Henry Cooke and on through Drew and "Roaring" Hanna, an assembly line of rabble-rousing preachers have often parlayed sermons into anti-Catholic riots.

The Orange Order filtered and infected the bloodstream of Ulster until the order became the power base of the province. It was the establishment, with absolute control over the moral ethic, the police, the political machinery, and the courts. The Grandmaster of a lodge was a power who could ensure the job and well-being of a family. Failure to join or bucking the Orange Order by an individual in a given neighborhood, trade, or village was impossible, and the free thought of men who believed themselves to be free was destroyed.

The Unionist Party was born out of an Orange Hall in 1885 in response to the first home rule threat. Unionists have since become the political arm of the order, able to apply the kinds of threats and pressure that resulted in a history of British appeasement to Ulster.

It is hard to tell where one ended and the other began, but the Orange Order, the Unionist Party, and the Protestant Church formed an unholy trinity that kept the province in a stranglehold.

Orangeism finds public expression in a series of annual rituals, medieval in character and ugly in concept. It erupts into life during "the marching season."

The tune is set by the Lambeg drum, an ancient Scottish weapon of psychological warfare. It is up to four feet thick and five feet in diameter and tattooed by bamboo canes lashed to the wrists of the drummer by leather straps. The sound of it was designed to throw fear into the heart of the foe. It does. When it is carried on long frenzied marches, the drummer's wrists are often slashed open by the leather and his blood spatters against the drumhead. Many a Catholic child was first introduced to terror by the cannonade of the Lambeg drum.

The wee province bursts out with hundreds of thousands of Union Jacks and Ulster flags from every loyal house. There is nothing to compare with it in all the Crown's domains. Festive archways are larded with slogans that tell the Ulster story. REMEMBER 1690 (the Boyne); NOT AN INCH (the border dispute); GOD SAVE THE QUEEN, GOD SAVE ULSTER (loyalty); ULSTER WILL FIGHT AND ULSTER WILL BE RIGHT (anti-home rule); IN GLORIOUS REMEMBRANCE (of some victory or the other over the Catholic); FOR GOD AND ULSTER; and, of course, NO SURRENDER (the eternal siege).

180

Parades are marched from one end of the province to the other, grim, humorless trampings of righteous wrath. The first of two grand climaxes comes on the twelfth of July to celebrate William's victory at the Boyne. Tens of dozens of Loyal Lodges converge on Belfast. Throughout the night bonfires blaze, the Pope is kicked in effigy, prayers are prayed and the old tunes cranked up and sung with swelling pride.

The standard of the lyrics gives an idea of just how far the people have been manipulated. Among the things the men of the Orange Order did not bring to their beloved province were literature, music, and art. They are the ones mainly responsible for the place being a cultural desert.

CROPPIES LIE DOWN
Poor Croppies, ye know that your sentence was come,
When you heard the dread sound of the Protestant drum.
In memory of William we hoisted his flag,
And soon the bright Orange put down the Green rag.

THE PROTESTANT BOYS
The Protestant boys are loyal and true,
Stout-hearted in battle, and stout-handed too:
The Protestant boys are true to the last,
And faithful and peaceful when danger has passed.

DERRY'S WALLS
. . . For blood did flow in crimson streams,
On many a winter's night.
They knew the Lord was on their side,
To help them in the fight.

. . . At last, at last with one broadside
Kind heaven sent them aid. . . .

A ROPE, A ROPE TO HANG THE POPE
A rope, a rope
Tae hang the Pope!
A pennyworth o' cheese
Tae choke him!
A pint o' lamp oil
Tae wrench it down
And a big hot give
Tae roast him!

When I was sick,
And very, very sick,
And very near a-dying,
The only thing that raised me up
Was to see
The old whore frying.

Or consider some of the poetry, this one by no means the worst of the lot.

Scarlet Church of all uncleanness,
Sink thou to deep abyss,
To the orgies of obsceneness
Where the hell-bound furies hiss;
Where thy father Satan's eye
May hail thee, blood-stained Papacy!

Harlot! Cease thy midnight rambles,
Prowling for the life of saints,
Henceforth sit in hellish shambles
Where the scent of murder taints
Every gale that passeth by,
Ogre, ghoul of Papacy!

Leading his lodge in solemn remembrance, the Grandmaster, white-gloved, sword in hand, walks reverently behind a Bible borne on velvet cushion, encased in glass and topped with a crown.

The banners of Loyal Lodge after Loyal Lodge swear temperance, allegiance, and loyalty: CARSON'S TRUE BLUES, DERRY'S DEFENDERS, STEAMFITTERS TOTAL TEMPERANCE, ACT OF COVENANT, LOYAL LADS OF LARNE. . . . Tribal brothers all banded together in black bowlers, black rolled umbrellas, and sashes are piped on through by a hundred bands taunting close to Catholic neighborhoods or through the middle of them, while Shankill and Sandy Row toughs dance headily alongside the marchers, swept up by the wine of might.

By the time they reach Finaghy Field they've slowed to a limp, and they sprawl about to hear the old harangues from the old haranguers.

The next day at Scarva a mock Battle of the Boyne is re-enacted, and a month later it happens all over again as they go on pilgrimage to Derry to celebrate the siege.

If times are bad and passions high and fears of livelihood consuming, it might all be topped off with a bit of rioting against the Catholics.

To continue to intimidate and debase one third of their nation, it is entirely necessary to live in the past. They will relive Boyne and Derry until they make their earthly departure, and then their sons will be brought to wear the sash their fathers wore. As the pilot preparing to land at Belfast Airport said over the loudspeaker, "We are about to land in Ulster. Set your watches back three hundred years."

182

THE REV. MARTIN SMYTH

In recent years, the standard operation of Ulster was derailed, convulsing the Unionist Party and the established institutions. The sudden glare of the international spotlight was focused on the province, throwing the old hell-raisers into a defensive posture. As groups splintered and realigned, a great measure of the credibility and power of the Orange Order declined.

Martin Smyth personifies the kind of preacher who gained entrance to the organization's high councils and to whom it has fallen to rehabilitate its shattered image.

His personal credo places him on the right-hand side of the far right. It is his belief that godliness manifests itself through industriousness, and that the Protestant community is the most industrious. Actually, as a Presbyterian he feels his own sect is more industrious than Methodists, Baptists, and Anglicans, but this disparity can be minimized because, with all the Protestant brothers united in the Orange Order, a great deal of Presbyterian industriousness is bound to rub off on them.

Smyth no longer trusts the British, and this circumstance brings about a rather interesting concept of what Ulster should be. An ideal status for Ulster would be that of an independent commonwealth that could legislate for itself and continue the old Unionist game. However, he holds that Ulster should continue to have the British Army on call. He considers himself personally of Northern Irish origin and of British nationality. Although loyalty to Britain is part and parcel of the Orange experience, he would prefer a completely independent Ulster to one completely unified with Britain, whose politicians are constantly selling them down some river or the other. Nonetheless, it would be a sticky wicket to declare independence and so sever the British connection. What Martin Smyth really wants is a special divine status for the divine Protestants of Northern Ireland.

In his pamphlet "The Battle for Northern Ireland" he weaves along a contorted, tortured path through a maze in which he "proves" how the Catholics have had all the better of it in Ulster in jobs, education, housing, and social services and how the Catholics have terrorized the Protestants for fifty years.

Martin Smyth is no tricky dodger. The man is the real article. He will look you squarely in the eye and tell you that nowhere are Catholics treated better than in Northern Ireland, and what is more, he believes it.

To maintain the unmaintainable and rationalize the unrational, he has embellished upon the Orange fantasy of a papal takeover. It is the Pope and his agents who have the real, total control over the Catholic population; the Pope's wishes and not those of the people that would be made to decide the future of Ireland.

It follows that this sixteenth-century hangover from Reformation and Counter Reformation is the issue that must be kept alive by the Orange Order, for without the anti-Catholic fantasy it would no longer have a valid reason to exist.

THE ORANGEMAN

To paraphrase the old Orange toast, all that goodness has been slammed, crammed, and jammed into them for so long that the severity of it is worn like a badge of pain.

It is not to say that all Ulstermen are this way. The Belfaster in particular can be a sporty, lusty, drinking man owning one of the best senses of black humor in the world.

The Bible brought a certain majesty to their language. Portions of it were often recited from memory during the day's many prayers. Ulster, as it is spoken, is a lovely tongue.

But the Bible has been used as an all-covering protective blanket, a patchwork of phrases to "prove" superiority and exalted status. It is used to cover inadequacies in intellectual development, in rendering reason to a situation begging for reason, in providing compassion to fellow humans desperate for compassion.

The totalitarian nature and medievalism of it all have stunted any chance for richness in cultural achievement and have squeezed the Ulster people onto a dark, narrow path of spiritual slavery.

SCARVA *The pageant must go on. A day after the glorious twelfth of July the tribes mass once more at Scarva Castle for the annual mock Battle of the Boyne. It is obvious who is on the white horse and who is on the black.*

They have all shown up dutifully, but by now they're apt to be a tad weary from a month of marching—and, after all, everyone knows how the battle is going to turn out as good King Billy and his lads chase James around the cow pasture.

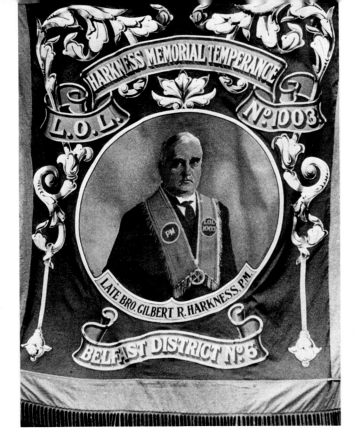

THE QUALIFICATIONS OF AN ORANGEMAN

Loyal Orange Institution of Ireland

The Master and members of every Lodge into which a candidate is proposed to be elected must satisfy themselves with all due solemnity previous to his admission that he possesses the following qualifications:

"An Orangeman should have a sincere love and veneration for his Heavenly Father; an humble and steadfast faith in Jesus Christ, the Saviour of mankind, believing in Him as the only Mediator between God and man. He should cultivate truth and justice, brotherly kindness and charity, devotion and piety, concord and unity and obedience to the laws; his deportment should be gentle and compassionate, kind and courteous; he should seek the society of the virtuous, and avoid that of the evil; he should honour and diligently study the Holy Scriptures, and make them the rule of his faith and practice; he should love, uphold, and defend the Protestant religion, and sincerely desire and endeavour to propagate its doctrines and precepts; he should strenuously oppose the fatal errors and doctrines of the Church of Rome, and scrupulously avoid countenancing (by his presence or otherwise) any act or ceremony of Popish worship; he should, by all lawful means, resist the ascendancy of that Church, its encroachments, and the extension of its power, ever abstaining from all uncharitable words, actions, or sentiments, towards his Roman Catholic brethren; he should remember to keep holy the Sabbath day, and attend the public worship of God, and diligently train up his offspring, and all under his control, in the fear of God, and in the Protestant faith; he should never take the name of God in vain, but abstain from all cursing and profane language, and use every opportunity of discouraging these, and all other sinful practices, in others; his conduct should be guided by wisdom and prudence, and marked by honesty, temperance, and sobriety; the glory of God and the welfare of man, the honour of his Sovereign, and the good of his country, should be the motive of his actions."

Sworn to wear the sash his father wore and thinking about all the things you have to be can just get a fellow down, sometimes.

We know when all is said,
We perish if we yield.
From *Ulster* by Rudyard Kipling

3. MOUNTING PASSIONS

For fifty years Northern Ireland was governed by the mon-olithic Unionist Party. It was the only game in town and the dice were loaded.

Some early attempts at parity soon vanished. Lord Craig-avon had held open a third of the newly formed Royal Ulster Constabulary for Catholics, but the attitude and atmosphere made it unattractive for them to join and be used as instru-ments of repression against their own people. From the begin-ning, the RUC and their B-Specials were Protestant to the bone. The Special Powers Act was invoked time and again in real and imagined emergencies, a constant sword of Damocles over Catholic heads.

In education, early attempts to integrate public schools met resistance from both sides, proving that the Hierarchy can be just as autocratic as the Orange Order.

An intrinsic Protestant fear is that of being outbred by the R.C.s. To insure political domination, the Unionists canceled out proportional representation in the electorate. It was a system that guaranteed minority equity and was the only fair way in a place where the ethnic make-up of the state is split along such distinct lines. Fairness was never part of the Unionist policy, and proportional representation met an early death.

In its place, gerrymandering of voting districts was instituted to insure to Unionists the lion's share of contested seats in those areas where the Catholics were in the majority. This bit of ingenuity is achieved by drawing up boundaries in such a manner that the Catholics may be jammed into a district whose vote can be matched by a Protestant district with half the population. In practical application, Dungannon, for example, has about a fifty-fifty Catholic/Protestant voter ratio, but the lines are drawn so that the Catholics usually end up with seven council seats while the Unionists come in with fourteen. In this universal Ulster system, Derry City is the worst: a sixty-eight per cent Catholic population has eight seats and a thirty-

two per cent Protestant electorate has twelve. Gerrymandering was further iced, until recent years, by a number of dual votes granted to certain classes of property and business owners who were overwhelmingly Protestant.

Those branches of the civil service that have been run from London, such as the Post Office and Inland Revenue, had some job parity at first, but the ratio eroded in time. In the civil service that has been run from Stormont, Protestants in govern-ment jobs came to around eighty-five per cent and upward, with a monopoly on all top positions and most of the top pay grades. Taking a look at the Stormont government itself, one sees that in 1961 the civil service fell into two categories, technical-professional and administrative. In the first instance there was a total of 209 employees, of which 13 were Catholic. In administration, of the 319 positions in all departments, 23 were held by Catholics. The totality of the injustice can be seen right on down the line in government hospitals, schools, the police, public boards, institutions, and services.

In public housing, the inequity was furthered by a Catch-22. Catholics were not permitted public housing in Protestant areas out of fear that it would change the voting balance of the gerrymandered districts. In Derry, the Catholics appear to have been fairly dealt with in numbers of new units, but what really happened was that they were jammed into an intolerable ghetto, the worst in the British Isles.

Private industry belonged to a single class. Jobs were an integral part of a silent conspiracy between the industrialist and the Orange/Unionist combine. Apprenticeships in the more desirable trades had to be purchased and were carefully handed down from father to son in Protestant families to shut off Catholic intrusion. The Catholic lot was, for the most part, that of small farmer, shopkeeper, and laborer, and the system was meticulously controlled. Certain areas of the province with large Catholic populations were deliberately allowed to stagnate

PATRICIA McCLUSKEY *once was a social worker in the worst slums of Catholic Glasgow, and the pain of it never went away. This Dungannon housewife became the mother of Civil Rights. She was the founder of the Homeless League and the Campaign for Social Justice, and the landmark exposé, "The Plain Truth," was born in a two-by-four office in her home. For eight years she fought it out on the city council and became a force for justice in Ulster politics. There seems to be a great deal of sorrow in her now. "I look back and wonder. I wonder if the violence could have been avoided."*

economically in order to drive them from Ulster and keep their numbers down.

There always were ways to determine a man's religion when it came to seeking a job, education, or housing in what has been perfectly described as an institutionalized caste system.

The British attitude remained one of acquiescence toward the Unionists. Britain had had her fill of problems with Republicans, and her natural sympathies lay with "her own kind" who were loyal. Unionist politicians allied with the Conservative Party wheedled support at every turn in exchange for their votes in Westminster. Ulster generally walked an economic tightrope, for much of her prosperity was artificial in nature, in the form of support from the British taxpayer.

The catalogue of injustices mounted and the rumbles of dissent could be heard clearly from the Catholic ghettos. By 1960, leaks began to spring in the Unionist ship. As Prime Minister, Terence O'Neill was somewhat more of a moderate than the Craigavon, Brookborough breed. He threw out a few crumbs. Not equality, but tokenism. Even that brought violent Protestant reaction. Inevitably, Civil Rights groups had formed and were on the march, and things would never be the same again. In the end, the Catholics of Northern Ireland had no choice but to rise against the regime.

DR. CON McCLUSKEY *"We did the right thing. We fought for jobs and housing." Con McCluskey considers himself a background pamphleteer to his wife's activities. In his spare time Dr. Con sculpts in metal in a tiny basement studio. Most of his works depict fellow human beings in agony and bondage.*

THE EDGE OF DARKNESS

When Civil Rights did come, the conspiracy was nothing more sinister than a group of middle-class housewives in Dungannon protesting the lack of housing allocations to low-income Catholics, some of whom had been waiting vainly for up to six years. They squatted in new units, marched, and went directly into local politics under the leadership of Mrs. Patricia McCluskey. Her Campaign for Social Justice was founded upon the Homeless League in 1964, and a pamphlet, "The Plain Truth," listing some of the hard, irrefutable facts of blatant injustice, was published soon after. "The Plain Truth" was a blockbuster.

The Civil Rights Association started in 1967 with a strong infusion from the left that emanated from Belfast's Queen's University campus. Bernadette Devlin was among their number.

Prime Minister Terence O'Neill's reform package was closing the barn door after the horse had long gone, but still it was considered by the Orange Order as giving dangerous concessions. The one man, one vote issue in particular frenzied the Protestants.

Civil Rights marches and harassment of the government increased throughout 1968, until further marches were banned.

In defiance of the ban, several thousand unarmed, nonviolent marchers were assaulted in Derry by a free-swinging baton charge of the Royal Ulster Constabulary, which sent a hundred Civil Righters to the hospital. But something new had been added. The RUC performance was carried out in full impersonal view of BBC television cameras, and a British public that literally knew nothing about Ulster was shocked and alarmed. Among the surprises was that this was considered "business as usual," the only way to keep Catholics in their place in a British province.

Terence O'Neill, reeling under the indignation, disbanded the loathed local government of Derry and replaced it with a commission, dismissed William Craig, and promised other reforms. In O'Neill's Unionist Party, support began to flake off with resignations of hard-liners.

It was a cinch to incite Protestant mobs, for now there was a Communist bogeyman to go along with fear of international Romanism. The year 1969 opened with a brutal attack by a mob armed with cudgels, brass knuckles, broken glass, and spiked clubs at Burntollet Bridge. As Civil Righters' skulls were cracked and they were flung into the river, the RUC looked the other way. Again, this was done on camera and now world attention was being won. Civil Rights marches met the same fate in Newry and elsewhere, the action of the Constabulary being consistently brutal in all cases.

In April a jolter came with the election of Bernadette Devlin to Westminster. In quick succession O'Neill's government fell and the B-Specials were mobilized. Major James Chichester-Clark, O'Neill's successor, simply was not the man to match the hour.

By the time the marching season rolled around, tension was peaking. During the twelfth of July parades, Catholics were baited unmercifully by the Orangemen as preface to Protestant riots in Belfast and Dungiven.

As Apprentice Boys Day on August 12 came into sight, the smell was in the air for a massive, province-wide anti-Catholic pogrom. Harold Wilson's Labour Government in London vacillated. He attempted to dupe the Unionists with the threat that if he sent in troops he would suspend Stormont and rule directly from London. It was a bluff calculated to make the Unionists cool things down themselves, for the last thing Wilson wanted was direct involvement from London.

A Junior Orangemen's Parade on August 2, ending with riots against the Catholic housing development of Unity Flats in Belfast, provided a foretaste of what was coming, yet the Chichester-Clark government hedged against banning the Apprentice Boys march in Derry. Constabulary Inspector General Peacocke felt he would be better able to deal with the parade than with the consequences of calling it off.

Derry's Catholic ghetto of Bogside had little doubt of what was going to happen and full well knew it was without police protection. A defense committee was organized and made ready.

The massive Constabulary and B-Specials cordoned off the Catholics as the parade swung dangerously close to Bogside. The Apprentice Boys were particularly vile on that day, shouting hostile obscenities, taunting with songs and curses, and showering pennies down on the ghetto from the wall above. Locked into their zoo, with three hundred years of British oppression and fifty years of Unionism behind them, the Catholics burst out in a rage of frustration and countered the Protestant torment with a barrage of rocks.

The Constabulary moved toward Bogside with an avenging Protestant mob behind them. The approaches to the ghetto turned into alleys of carnage as the police were greeted from rooftops with thousands of petrol bombs, stones, and slings. The B-Specials, literally untrained for riot work and effective mainly as a bully force, proved unequal to the situation. CS gas, a cousin of mace, was poured into the ghetto behind Constabulary armor, but the Catholics had stopped them cold and were dealing out heavy casualties. As the Battle of the Bogside raged, brush fires in Belfast, Armagh, Dungiven, Dungannon, and

Coalisland erupted.

In Belfast the rioting reached epic proportions. In the Ardoyne, an isolated Catholic enclave, nearly two hundred Catholic homes were gutted by fire, and refugees and casualties began to number in the thousands. The RUC went trigger-happy and on "suspicion" machine-gunned Unity Flats indiscriminately.

Within forty-eight hours it was apparent the police could not contain the situation. In Derry alone they had taken two hundred and fifty casualties and were to take nearly a thousand before the summer was out. The Catholics in Bogside had battled them to a state of exhaustion.

On August 19, British General Freeland took command of all forces. For the first time in their sordid history, the Unionists were not in control of their own fate.

The Constabulary and B-Specials limped out of Bogside to be replaced by British troops, marking the beginning of the end of the disgraceful reign.

Discredited for their ugly, uneven sectarian behavior, the B-Specials were disarmed by the British and Inspector General Peacocke was replaced by the police commissioner of London.

The end of the summer saw two reports filed by British commissions that shocked Protestant Ulster down to its jackboots.

The Cameron Report reiterated Catholic grievances in no uncertain terms. The carefully cloistered Unionist operation was now on public display. Exposed were the rigged election boundaries, discrimination in jobs and housing, deaf ears to legitimate complaints, the existence of suppressive paramilitary forces, and the Special Powers Act.

The Hunt Commission Report on the police was even more damning. It recommended disbanding the B-Specials, disarming the Royal Ulster Constabulary, and repealing the Special Powers Act.

The Protestants, enraged by the sudden fall of their sacred cows, took instantly to rioting again. They blamed Communists for Civil Rights and the IRA for the Battle of Bogside. CRA —Civil Rights Association—in their lexicon stood for Communist, Romanist Agitation.

British troops were now pouring in. At first the Catholics welcomed them as a peace force, but that illusion was soon to end. The Protestants had other ideas. After all, the British Army had always been "their" army.

Chichester-Clark was out and Brian Faulkner, a no-nonsense Unionist who was deaf in both ears to Catholics and Civil Rights, was the new Prime Minister. The Conservative Party was now in power in London and it was the traditional ally of the Unionists.

If there was ever a time to make the moves to create peace, this was it. Yet what was totally beyond Unionist/Protestant comprehension was the ability to recognize legitimate complaints against injustice and brutality. With the British Army in tow and Stormont well and alive, the Unionists and Protestants were to act in the only way they ever had acted; this time they were backed with water cannons, CS gas, rubber bullets, and, if needed, lead ones.

The new militant posture of the Catholics was blamed on the IRA, which, in fact, had long been a dormant and impotent force. The IRA indeed was reborn out of the events of the summer of 1969, but those most directly responsible for the rebirth were the Orange Order, the Unionist Party, and the Royal Ulster Constabulary.

BERNADETTE

Bernadette Devlin was born into a large, impoverished Catholic family from Cookstown in County Tyrone. Her first appearance on the public scene was at Queen's University in Belfast in the company of socialist students during the Civil Rights movement in 1967. She was there at that first march in Derry in October 1968, which met with a baton charge from the Royal Ulster Constabulary televised to a shocked British public.

Bernadette was there at Burntollet Bridge when the Ian Paisley mob assaulted the unarmed marchers with bottles, clubs, stones, and crowbars. "One Paisleyite swung a huge plank at me and I still remember it coming towards my eyes with two big nails sticking out. I threw my hands across my face and the nails drove into the backs of my hands . . . then the man slammed me across the knees, and I fell to the ground. Four or five of his mates gathered around me, trying to kick my face in. I curled into a ball, covering my head with my arms, while boots slammed into me."

She was there at Apprentice Boys Day when the blood-thirsty taunts of the Orange mob spiraled into the Battle of Bogside. Exhorting women to build barricades, exhorting the men not to crack, she hurled stones until she could not lift her arm.

She was there on the speaker's rostrum at Free Derry Corner when the paratroopers gunned down a peaceful assembly in the horror to become known as Bloody Sunday.

Though she is tiny and drab, her tongue lashes out like a yard of vinegar at her enemies. A maverick in her personal life, she ignores the hyprocrisy of the "holy" establishment.

Bernadette Devlin was voted into Commons at the age of twenty-one, one of the youngest ever. Photographed in mini-skirt and depicted by the British press as "the swinging M.P. from Mid-Ulster," she was anything but that, and her comet rose wildly for the moment. By the end of 1969 the left-wing power of the Civil Rights movement had petered out, reduced to tired rhetoric and unending pamphlets. Her unabated anger will be remembered by the physical assault on Reginald Maudling, the Home Secretary, who was putting the official line on Bloody Sunday in the House of Commons.

The dream of unity of Catholic and Protestant in a workers' paradise is ideal enough, but its execution through her politics remains on the far side of reality, most of it incompatible with Irish and Ulster nature.

She is no longer a member of Parliament but, nonetheless, Bernadette Devlin has earned immortality as a magnificent champion of her people and the most dynamic symbol of a dynamic era.

IAN R. K. PAISLEY—Portrait of a Demagogue

The most diabolical by-product of three hundred and fifty years of the plantation of Ulster is a cancerous growth known as Paisleyism. Ian Richard Kyle Paisley was born in Armagh in 1926, the son of a Baptist minister who ordained him only twenty years later, after minimal studies, and so commenced a chapter bizarre even for Northern Ireland.

Few men possess the power to hate with such magnitude, and, more frightening, few have the energy and ability to transmit and infect fellow creatures with that hatred.

As shrewd as he is ruthless, Paisley discovered flaws in his society that could readily be exploited. He broke early from the formal Church, founding his own rump sect, the Free Presbyterians, which, incidentally, have no standing in world Presbyterianism. Establishing himself as Moderator, he had no rules to obey or theological authority to answer to in his relentless drive for power.

His stock in trade is playing on the most primal fears of lower-middle-class Orange mentality. He established himself as a superstar, with masterful elocution and robed in a unique Reformation cassock. In his outdoor meetings he wore a distinctive white coat that set him apart.

Snubbed by the Anglo/Ulster Ascendancy, he made off to America to gain some academic credentials. From Bob Jones University, a fundamentalist Bible school, he learned the fine arts of gospel evangelism.

His role is that of the Reformation man reincarnated to save Protestantism from another Inquisition or St. Bartholomew's Massacre, and what better place than Ulster. On the Battle of the Boyne he roared from his pulpit:

"God raised up Oliver Cromwell . . . when puritanism came in and, with it, all the floodtide of holiness. . . .

"The fruits of democracy are the direct fruits of Reformation . . . where Rome rules there is not only religious tyranny but political tyranny. . . . The first Protestant Bishop of Liverpool said let the dog return to its vomit . . . let the Israelite return to Egyptian bondage but let no Englishman with brains ever suggest we should return to pre-Reformation days for these days would be days of darkness, days of intolerance and days of the vilest priestly tyranny . . . you can't have liberty and have a Popish monarchy . . . all the tyranny flowed from one quarter and that quarter was Vaticanism. . . .

". . . all that is best in a free democracy, all that is best from the highest standards of British liberty flows . . . directly from the Battle of the Boyne . . . a battle that has its repercussions to this day.

". . . as an arrow straight to its target the forces of William drove their way into the heart of the enemy. James the Second, who had no stomach for the fight . . . turned his horse and sped . . . which was the end of the dynasty of a Roman Catholic monarchy in these islands and please God . . . never again a Popish prince mount the throne of Britain and never again Popish tyranny rule. . . .

". . . the battle was one of truth against the lie, of tyranny against freedom. One of Bible Protestantism against all the vileness of Papal abominations . . . you sit in this house tonight and you worship God in simple Reform fashion for that great victory and you today have special privileges . . . Freedom! Freedom! Glorious freedom!

". . . there are forces in this province this night who would like, by the same despotic tyranny, to take from you your hard wrought freedom, to steal and filch from you the privileges that are yours because of your forefather's sacrifice."

Paisley's public performance is about as subtle as a rhino, and like the rhino, which is nearsighted, he will trample anything within reach.

Like the rhino, his skin is of armor, and he glories in being reviled. He often land-mines his own path deliberately to gain attention and sympathy, and for years there was a yearning for the martyrdom of imprisonment. He finally got his wish by pushing the authorities beyond the breaking point. Paisley was able to bathe in glory with weekly messages from prison cell to congregation.

I've been in the prison cell twice for my principles. . . . I've mingled with murderers and those who have fallen deep into the troughs of sin. . . . I was locked in my cell for hours on end and I can testify today that Jesus gave me peace. . . . I walked in the valley of the shadows and my life was attacked and an attempt was made to poison me by one who was the emissary of the Roman Catholic Church. . . .

199

Fresh from his triumphant visit to Crumlin Road Jail in 1966, he had bestowed on him an honorary Doctorate of Divinity from Bob Jones University, topped with a grand tour of Scotland and the Bible belt of America.

Playing no favorites, he bestows his hate on a wide, cultivated range of enemies. Captain Terence O'Neill came under particular denunciation as a traitor because of a visit by the Irish Prime Minister, Sean Lemass. The Duke of Edinburgh, no less, was highly suspect for his Greek birth and Orthodox baptism.

On the death of Pope John, when most decent Christians mourned, Paisley voiced disgust over "Protestant concern at the lying eulogies now being paid to the Roman Antichrist by non-Romanist Church leaders." If there is any issue that enrages the Moderator it is the ecumenical movement, and he denounces the World Council of Churches. Billy Graham has been denounced as a papal agent for his open-minded approach to the same ecumenical movement. Paisley's fundamentalism considers any version of the Bible other than King James a blasphemy and a perversion, and he has no place for a world brotherhood among Christians.

Ecumenism is doctrinally unbiblical . . . basically unprotestant . . . ecclesiastically unclean . . . practically unChristian . . . spiritually untrustworthy . . . it includes membership of the Greek Orthodox Church which plunges to the depths of the basest idolatries and is a Bible-hating church . . . the Archbishop of Canterbury would welcome the Pope as chairman and seems to be eager to slobber on the Pope's slippers.

He has shown up in protest at Lambeth Palace, home of the Archbishop of Canterbury, and made an exhibition of himself

200

in Rome, where he was drummed out of the country and advised never to return.

Paisley's platform appearances outside his church are carefully staged, with an elite corps of toughs to do the hatchet jobs from the audience. Major Ronald Bunting, a mathematics teacher whom Paisley "saved," commanded his followers for Paisley's marches. More than one distinguished visiting churchman was howled from the stage for daring to hold an opinion other than Paisley's "true gospel."

Paisley found his great issue when the Civil Rights movement came into being. He relentlessly exploited the fears of the Protestants in the period following the brutality at Burntollet Bridge through the awful summer of 1969, when his rabble rousing bottomed to an all-time low.

> I hate the system of Roman Catholicism, but God being my judge, I love the poor dupes who are ground down under that system. Particularly I feel for their Catholic mothers who have to go out and prostitute themselves before old bachelor priests.

His most notable victory was attained in collapsing the O'Neill government over Civil Rights and getting himself elected to both Stormont and Westminster. At Westminster, Paisley brilliantly adjusted his style to a new audience—it is hard to believe that the witty and candid M.P. is the same man as the apocalyptic evangelist of Belfast. The new Paisley has effectively won over thousands in Ulster, Britain, and even Ireland.

In support of a most remarkable Jekyll and Hyde charade, his Puritan Press runs overtime with a nonstop barrage of hate literature.

> They [the Jesuits] by character assassination seek to silence every voice raised in exposure of their aims. Where they have power they remove by murder of their opponents. They are adept in the use of the poisoned cup and poignard. . . .

To watch Paisley in action on the pulpit is a sobering experience. A spellbinding orator with the full bag of catch phrases and gimmickry, he plunges into a well-orchestrated performance with lights, sound, and music that would make Elmer Gantry look like a piker. In short order the plastic flowers on the women's straw hats are quivering with fear, and the guts of the square-cut gentlemen are churning with transplanted hate.

Gazing on his flock with detached contempt, Paisley treats them as though they were children. He knows what frightens them and where their nerves are raw, and his thunderbolts are simplified and lean and aimed straight for the twin targets of heart and jugular vein.

In the end he lets them know about his own fraternal relationship with God; he and he alone stands as friend between them and Jesus.

> I have known the peace of God . . . God gives peace. I have known a peace that is calm as a river, a peace that the sons of this world never knew, and do you know what my prayer is? That you'll get peace today . . . you need help. . . .
> . . . if you are saved, that's all that matters. We walk on a knife's edge. No one knows who next in this congregation will fall to the assassins' bullet . . . we walk on the knife's edge, every one of us. You need to be ready, man, for the call to the great eternity. Thank God you can be ready tonight. The door of grace is open. . . .

After the backsliders and the sinners have crawled into his office to be taken to Christ by him and after the silent collection (no silver, only paper), he is likely to throw them a crumb to assure his continued hold. He lets them in on something God has revealed to him.

> And God has shown me He has a remnant of people in Ulster. He has His own people here. A chosen people! An elect people! A redeemed people! A blood-washed people! A saved people! A God-fearing people! A separated people! His people! And I believe God!

To the outside observer, Ian Paisley's religious leadership is remarkably similar to that of his chosen enemy. He has created his own hegemony in some dozen free Presbyterian churches. His own Martyrs' Memorial claims the largest attendance in the British Isles, and he, Paisley, is the Moderator, with authority and charisma that might be envied in Rome. He uses it with a totalitarianism that few Catholic churchmen practice.

But Ian Paisley's hour is passing. Politically he is isolated on the far right. Major Bunting has deserted the fold. The struggle has become one in which guns are more important than oratory.

But these are moments of infamy, and all Ulster still trembles at Paisley's wrath. If a man could be singled out as responsible for the tragic condition of Northern Ireland, no one has more to answer for than Ian Paisley.

Dr. Con McCluskey has said he always felt that Jesus would have sat among the squatters seeking decent housing in Dungannon. That is probably true. What is even more true is that Jesus would not have been waiting in ambush at Burntollet Bridge with a club in his hands.

BY AUTHORITY OF THE SPECIAL POWERS ACT . . .

The year 1970 opened with a lick and a promise but avalanched toward disaster from then on. The B-Specials were disbanded on March 26. A steady input of British troops brought their number to over ten thousand, ostensibly as a peace-keeping force. The Protestant population took the army's presence to mean what it had always meant in Ulster, that they were on loan to Stormont to put the "croppies" down.

An army functioning as a police force inevitably invites disaster. A police constable is an ordinary part of daily life, and when he makes an arrest it is generally considered the act of a lawman doing his job. A soldier in battle dress with armor and battlefield weapons performing the same task conjures up an entirely different meaning.

With memories of the 1969 riots clear in Catholic minds, with the mass influx of British troops into civilian areas, and with another Orange marching season coming up, recruitment for the revitalized IRA was in full swing. In those abysmal ghettos, where per capita income was seldom over poverty level and where unemployment ran twenty per cent and more, the

IRA appeal found ready takers. During this period the IRA had split into two factions. The Provisionals, or Provos, being the traditional, larger, and more militant wing, while the Officials were politically oriented, with leanings to the left. The battle was mainly fought by the Provos.

Early in the year British soldiers on patrol were treated matter-of-factly by Catholics. It was no sin to fraternize or invite the lads in for tea. As IRA ranks filled and incidents mounted, the army adopted "get tough" measures. The new order of the day was raids upon arms caches—swift swoops and "search and destroy" tactics. "Dustbin brigades" of women clanging garbage-can tops on the pavement to warn of troops in the area followed nonfraternization, flare-ups, and rising tension.

The army's even-handed façade melted, if indeed it was ever truly even-handed. Protestants urged the army to be more aggressive. Disbanded B-Specials had re-formed into "rifle clubs," and an illegal paramilitary organization, the Ulster Volunteers, strutted more and more openly. A new Northern Irish unit of the British Army, the Ulster Defense Regiment, militia

HER MAJESTY'S PRISON, THE MAZE *Called "Silver City" by the British Army and "Dachau" by the Catholics, the Maze has become the dreaded symbol of the Internment policy under the Special Powers Act. The agony of the Maze erupted in October 1974 when the inmates rioted and burned most of it down. It was quickly restored to full operation.*

in character, was tantamount to being totally Protestant.

On the political front, Edward Heath and the Conservatives had come into power in London. Long-overdue reforms were left lying fallow, a circumstance that only served to substantiate the Catholic case that they were being betrayed once more. Subsequent IRA actions brought on an escalating counteraction from the army, and so by the end of the summer of 1970 there was a complete split between British forces and the Catholics.

Early 1971 found Chichester-Clark coming under heavy pressure from the reactionary elements of the Unionist Party to stop reforms and to bring in more British troops. The pressure peaked in March, when three young Scottish soldiers were executed and the blame was laid on the IRA, although this was never proved.

It was enough, however, to send Chichester-Clark packing off to see Heath under threat of a Protestant backlash. Among his demands were more troops to move in and occupy Catholic areas. In one of the few illuminated decisions Heath made, he refused, thus turning his back on a Unionist ally. It brought on Chichester-Clark's resignation, which didn't faze Heath at this juncture.

Brian Faulkner, a hard-line, bedrock Unionist, took over. He was not of the gentry, as O'Neill and Chichester-Clark were, but he had wealth from the family textile fortunes. It has been said of Faulkner, "He may not be able to dance on the head of a pin, but he can certainly maneuver in tight quarters." His greatest political attribute has been expediency. Heath, in fact, in trading off the devil he knew for the devil he didn't know, had ended up with a disastrous bargain.

Faulkner had been Ulster Minister of Home Affairs in the O'Neill government and had resigned, protesting against rights for Catholics. His ascendance to Prime Minister was greeted fearfully by the Catholic community. He made an early pass at some sort of accommodation, but it had come decades late and his intentions were mistrusted. The IRA bomb campaign was heating up rapidly, and Faulkner's presence did little to deter it. In those early days, before violence had become an hourly occurrence and a way of life, each bomb strike or IRA raid made a heavy impact. Blood was now being drawn on a regular basis, and each new Catholic death brought on a martyr's funeral of grief-stricken, enraged mass processions.

By midsummer of 1971 the army no longer posed as a peace-keeping force but inched toward full-scale operations against the IRA/Catholic enemy. Army options were being considered. An "enemy" list of sorts had been assembled, and the smell of Internment was in the air.

In early August, Faulkner and the new commanding general, Harry Tuzo, went to London for consultations. Heath's government was bereft of policy or contingency plans. Every-

one, including Tuzo, was wary of getting involved with Internment, but no one seemed to have any alternatives. Certainly no one opted for immediate reforms to alleviate the situation. Faulkner finally pleaded the Internment case as the only answer, and a perplexed and somewhat naïve British Cabinet took the bait.

The subsequent sweeps for suspects were Stalinist in character and Gestapo in execution. The IRA had sensed coming Internment and were prepared fairly well to do some fancy dodging during the roundups. Among the hundreds dragged in, there were some IRA people, but the majority were sympathizers, Civil Righters, old Republicans, and total innocents.

Doors were kicked in by boot and gun butt in the traditional middle-of-the-night strikes, men were beaten and dragged half naked before the eyes of their children and hysterical wives, furniture was smashed up and windows broken. Interrogations, which came under scrutiny of a British commission, deplored their own army's brutality. By the end of 1971 nearly one thousand men had been salted away for indefinite terms without charges against them and without legal rights.

Far from putting the violence to an end, the sweeps opened the floodgates. Moderate Catholics now flocked to the IRA, and hatred of the British became as intense as at any time in their centuries of occupation. Edward Heath and his Home Secretary, Reginald Maudling, had been led down the garden path by Brian Faulkner into a catastrophe. In all of England's history as empire builder and colonizer, one would have to search hard to duplicate the blunder of Internment.

4. FLASH POINT DERRY

The City of Londonderry is now compassed about with a very strong wall, excellently made and neatly wrought, being all of good lime and stone; the circuit whereof is two hundred and eighty-four perches and two-thirds, at eighteen feet to the perch; besides the four gates which contain eighty-four feet, and in every place of the wall is twenty-four feet high and six feet thick.

This report, written in 1618, marks the beginning of Ulsterism, the imposition of poverty on the native population finally climaxed by fifty years of Unionism in its most perverse, corrupt, and evil form. Derry personifies the ills and symbolizes the struggle like no other place.

The foundations were religious. Columba founded Derry through the establishment of a monastery in 546 and the spirit of that beloved saint has given it a deeply Catholic character.

The O'Neill Clan remained unconquered by the Normans and were the power in Ulster until the "Flight of the Earls" after the O'Neills' defeat at Kinsale in 1602. Their departure from the scene signaled the plantation of Ulster, the wholesale land grab by the Ascendancy, and the importation of the Scottish Presbyterians.

To defend the western reaches, Derry was given to a consortium of London guilds and merchants to exploit it commercially and establish it as a crown fortress. Its parent organization went under the improbable name of the Honourable Irish Society, and the name London was combined with that of Derry, the Celtic word for oak. To this day it is referred to by all Catholics and many Protestants simply as Derry. It was the very first English colony.

Completion of the wall established a central theme of Ulsterism: "defense against the siege." The defenses were to come into play shortly with Derry's vaunted wall holding back the Peasants' Rising of 1641, and several years later in the Owen Roe O'Neill and Cromwell wars. In each instance Protestants from the surrounding countryside crammed into the walled city to save themselves from native wrath.

Derry's epic of glory was reached in 1689 when James II, in attempting to regain the British throne, set up operations in Ireland and part of his forces under Lord Antrim moved on

207

Edgy British armor on patrol in the ominous quiet before dusk.

BOGSIDE *The column immortalizing Mayor Walker looks down on century-and-a-half-old housing gutted in recent years of rioting. The statue of Walker was unceremoniously removed by an IRA bomb.*

DERRY'S WALL *Looking down on Bogside, scene of penny throwing and a spawning ground of riots.*

Derry. It looked as though they were going to be able to march right on in when thirteen Derry Apprentice Boys shut Bishop's Gate, locking them out. The siege began.

James's forces had neither sufficient artillery to breach the wall nor infantry with the arms and stamina to make a direct assault. A boom was dropped across the river Foyle to cut off relief from the sea. For over three months the blockade wrought havoc on the defenders, who lost thousands by disease and starvation. Relief ships finally made their appearance, and the blast that broke the boom and lifted the siege has been lionized along with the Apprentice Boys. Derry now assumed its second religious character, that of the holy city of Protestant Ulster.

The siege of 1689 has never really been lifted. From the onset, Catholics were unwelcome within the walls and were made to settle in boglands outside. Their little hovels always look up to the walls and to the column glorifying the Rev. George Walker, the mayor during the siege. They bred in unsanitary mud-streeted hovels, each with its postage-stamp yard for the raising of a hog and a potato patch.

From its beginning as a textile town, Derry has been a place of female and child labor. Men languished in apathy, a quarter of their work force perennially unemployed.

For Catholics it has always been a place of despair. They were the stoop labor force, kept at existence level through the penal days, and they fell below that level during the famine. Blessed relief came through death in the streets, the terrifying workhouses, orphanages, and fever hospitals. Drinking, brawling, begging, pawning to the debt limit, and seasonal emigration were the standard of life. Permanent emigration drained off the vitality of the community.

When partition came, the Unionist/Orange/Protestant supremacy clique demanded that Londonderry, their Jerusalem, be included in Northern Ireland. This was accomplished despite the fact that the population was two thirds Catholic, that Derry belonged to Donegal economically, and that its seizure amputated it from its natural life's blood. Gerrymandering of the voting districts was established so that the minority had political control over the majority in what was the worst excess of its kind in Ulster.

What followed then was an exercise by the Unionists in economic genocide. The jobs lost by Derry's separation from

209

Donegal were never replaced. Rail lines were cut. Traditional shipping lines to Glasgow and other trading ports ceased operation. After World War II the shipbuilding industry was shut down. The docks and shipyards deteriorated through stagnation.

Male unemployment reached staggering proportions as the city remained a place of cheap female labor in the shirtmaking factories. The O'Neill government initiated grandiose plans to lure outside capital to Ulster and increase the province's manufacturing capacity. It seemed obvious that the place to infuse jobs would be Derry, but the Unionists had other ideas. As a vicious body blow, the new industrial complex of Craigavon was created in the eastern part of the province to further the prosperity of the Protestant majority in that area. Derry's Catholics were left to die.

The greatest single obscenity the Unionists imposed was shutting down Magee University, one of two in Ulster, and removing the campus to the Protestant-dominated city of Coleraine. This was the first case in the history of Western civilization of the arbitrary political closing of a university in this manner.

Along with the economic strangulation, the housing situation was desperate. The first half dozen years of any marriage had to be spent in substandard housing. Children were born into a condition reflecting the depression and trauma of the parents. The majority of children were never to know any other kind of home.

When the housing situation was alleviated in the 1960s, it was done with customary Unionist duplicity. The Creggan Estate bordering Bogside was kept in a single ward so as not to upset the voting balance. Creggan and Bogside became massive ghettos, with the Catholics locked in. When land ran out, the Unionists erected a vertical slum, the Rossville Flats, built over Meenan Park, the only playing field in the area.

With it all they descended on each Apprentice Boys Day with their Lambeg drums, their marching bands, their banners, their slogans, and their humiliating bravado. It is small wonder that Derry and the man-made hell of Bogside have been the leading edge of the hurricane.

Siege within a siege. A Protestant street in a Catholic area buttons up with banners flying defiantly for God and Ulster.

DERRY STREET SCENES

JOHN HUME—A Voice in the Wilderness

John Hume was born in Derry in 1937, the first of seven children. His father went without work from the end of World War II until his death twenty years later. Augmenting the slim wages of his mother and the unemployment payments, he started to work at the age of eight. His memories are of life in crammed quarters and lots of pork disguised in many manners. Pork was the staple and bane of the Derry Catholic, including minced pork, made up of the butcher's leavings.

He decided against priesthood after three years at Maynooth, where he earned degrees in French and modern history. Returning home, he taught school for ten years, became involved in social work, and researched a brilliant master's thesis on the social and economic history of Derry.

John Hume is a nonviolent man troubled over the fate of his people. His first fight was an attempt to reverse the scourge of defeatism. In a bootstrap operation, he started a communal self-help credit union with five pounds, and it grew to great success.

He wandered into politics inadvertently, but he seemed predestined to do so because of his position in the community. He led the protest march to Stormont over the closing of Magee University. A Civil Rights movement mushroomed shortly after and rendezvoused at Craigavon Bridge with the Royal Ulster Constabulary baton charge.

The Constabulary violence led directly to disbanding the odorous city hall operation and replacing it by a commission.

Hume had a general Irish disdain of politics and politicians but realized it was the most direct path to achieving social justice and he stood for Stormont and won.

Hume's road has been the grind of negotiation, in contrast to the IRA's violence, which he deplores and whose motives he doubts. His penetrating understanding of every element in the Ulster conflict has made him the best political brain on the island. He is a dedicated, unshakable man who is beyond personal intimidation, and there's been a fair measure of that from all sides. With his colleagues, Gerry Fitt and Paddy Devlin in Belfast, and the distinguished moralist Civil Righter Austin Currie, he has forged the Social Democratic Labor Party. They are far and away the most illuminating lights in Ulster politics.

Hume has proved to be a brilliant constitutionalist of the Parnell mold, time and again forcing the British to race for their lawbooks. The man most instrumental in getting the B-Specials disbanded, he compelled Westminster to pass overnight legislation to "legalize" the presence of the army.

"The Unionists are in a terrible trap. A situation created through injustice and living by injustice cannot survive the creation of justice. This was the strength of the Civil Rights movement because when it asked a question of the Unionist monolith . . . 'all we want is justice' it was a request they couldn't refuse, and when some of them tried to give it, obviously the whole structure began to fall apart."

When the bomber, the sectarian murder squad, and the bayonet have had their day, it will fall to the John Humes to bring sanity to a place that has known poor little of it.

LONDONDERRY AIR

After the Battle of Bogside, the IRA Provos came under command of Martin McGuinness, a twenty-two-year-old butcher's apprentice.

With the support of the civilian population, a small guerrilla unit can effectively tie up thousands of conventional forces. In the cesspool of Bogside and its Creggan satellite, most Catholics didn't care whether or not Derry was leveled to the ground.

The IRA's cat-and-mouse tactics slipped them through impossible cordons. Another day, audaciously, they'd show up at public rallies and funerals in clear-cut challenge to the authorities. They became precise in the use of gelignite. All revolutionaries make their own rules, and with the IRA a bombing was always preceded by a warning phone call.

Derry's commercial center was systematically devastated in a campaign designed to cripple business. Although warnings cut down on loss of life, the unending evacuations, daily bombings, sniping at troops, highjackings, and hit-and-run raids turned life into a prolonged nightmare. For a period during 1971–72 they were able to create Free Derry, an autonomous area that was avoided by British Army and Royal Constabulary alike.

The British Army's Operation Motorman temporarily dispersed the IRA in July 1972, but the continued absence of a settlement has brought them filtering back and into action. Although the people are weary, they still have no belief in Westminster's good intentions. The IRA will get support, either voluntarily or coerced, until that long-overdue day on which real justice makes its debut.

Esoterically and symmetrically set on the river Foyle, the picturesque first look belies the rage within.

BLOODY SUNDAY

Flash point Derry edged toward an inevitable explosion as 1972 approached. Internment had triggered massive civil disobedience. Bogside and Creggan were on a rent and rate strike, withholding public-housing payments from the government. The Catholic ghetto was ringed with army outposts and the Constabulary no longer entered. Barricading themselves in, Bogside and Creggan were virtual "no go" areas by the end of 1971.

William Street, a main artery from Bogside to the commercial center, had been bombed clean by the IRA, who controlled Free Derry. Stone and nail-bomb throwing became a daily event against troops on the William Street funnel.

Marches had been banned throughout the province by the end of 1971, but in defiance an anti-Internment demonstration was called for Sunday, January 30, 1972.

The Constabulary felt it would be too dangerous to prevent the march. The army then set up plans to contain it in the ghetto by the erection of twenty-six barricades of concrete slabs and barbed wire.

There was a second, secret plan, which called for a sweep into the ghetto to make mass arrests. Reinforcements were moved into Derry. Among them was 1 Para, the First Paratroop Battalion, as disciplined and elite a force as the British owned; to them fell the secret sweep operation. There can be little doubt that the British meant business on January 30.

As the crowd, numbering thousands, with women and children among them, gathered in Creggan, it was a rare day of sunshine. A jovial "Fair Day" atmosphere prevailed as the marchers moved in disarray through Bogside toward William Street and the Guildhall. The British contended that their massive presence was to prevent "hooligans" and IRA "gunmen" from taking over the rally. At the British barricades along William Street, the demonstrators were prodded back. Parade stewards tried to veer the marchers back to Free Derry Corner, and most of the people did turn around and occupy the large open ground, milling about rather aimlessly.

At the barricades a hundred or so younger people opened up on the troops by throwing stones, and rioting broke out. The troops answered with CS gas, rubber bullets, and purple-dye streams from a water cannon. By four o'clock the rioting had died out and it appeared to be universally accepted that the march would not make Guildhall. Speakers were on the platform at Free Derry Corner, and as Bernadette Devlin was announced as the first speaker the crowd edged toward her.

At that moment 1 Para moved in with armor and precision and opened fire on the assembly. The shooting lasted for more than a half hour. When it was over, thirteen civilians had been murdered and ten wounded.

Hitherto, aloof British tribunals for Ulster had knuckle-rapped the little brother province across the water. Fair play and all that. On this occasion, however, British troops were involved in a massacre of civilians. Lord Chief Justice Widgery conducted a one-man tribunal, and a much-criticized classic emerged in the form of the Widgery Report.

For openers, Lord Widgery stated that, had the law been respected, there would have been no parade and no one would have been killed. His lordship, however, didn't go quite far enough back, for if the British had given justice to Ulster's Catholics and had not invoked fascism through Internment, no protest would have been required.

The basis of the army's justification is a claim that it came under heavy fire and essentially acted in self-defense. The tribunal was required to reveal certain facts that damned the army's contentions.

Despite the alleged "assault" by the IRA, no British soldier was killed or wounded.

1 Para's orders were entirely vague, and the so-called riot area was completely peaceful at the time of their arrival.

Major General Ford, commander of the land forces, testified to the sniper theme, but even though he had come to Derry for the occasion, he was out of communication with his commanders.

Did 1 Para simply run amuck? Hardly. Although the area was flooded with women and children, their targets were amazingly selective. Half of those shot down were teen-agers, most likely facsimiles of what the typical IRA gunman is supposed to look like.

Did the Paras come under the fusillade they testified to? Not under any fusillade fired by the victims. No doubt some individual IRA men did shoot back. But there was never a shred of evidence to the effect that the IRA had any co-ordinated plan or that they opened fire first.

On what possible authority did 1 Para open fire? Each soldier carries a "yellow card" stating the conditions under which he is allowed to fire live ammunition. The instructions were clearly violated in that they ordered minimum force and shooting only in extreme conditions.

What was the truth behind British intentions on Bloody Sunday? There can be little doubt, from the manner of the movement of the Paras, that it was a planned operation. At a minimum, they were out to show the whip to the natives, to rough them up, knock over a few "hooligans," and leave Bogside to think things over.

There is a prevalent thesis that 1 Para opened fire on the crowd in a deliberate attempt to draw the IRA into the open and thus destroy it with a single blow. Had this tactic worked, the army would have been able to justify the death of civilians by also producing IRA gunmen's bodies.

The British deny any such intentions. However, one has to look no further than their press statements of the day after the massacre, in which they set out a detailed account showing that everyone who was killed had opened fire or thrown a bomb. 1 Para, according to their press release was only defending itself.

The Widgery tribunal was unable to substantiate that a single one of the murdered men carried arms or belonged to the IRA. Detailed medical examination of the bodies determined that most of them were shot in the back trying to escape the British gunmen.

A week earlier a headlined front-page article had appeared in the *Guardian*. This telling story has since been forgotten in the aftermath of Bloody Sunday.

Tuesday January 25 . . . COs WANT PARAS RESTRAINED. From Simon Hoggart in Belfast.

At least two British Army units in Belfast made informal requests to brigade headquarters for the Parachute Regiment to be kept out of their areas. Senior officers in these units regard the paratroops' tactics as too rough and on occasions, brutal. One officer in a troubled area, whose commanding officer made such a request, said: "The paratroops undid in 10 minutes community relations which it has taken us four weeks to build up."

News of the requests, which to say the least is extraordinary within the British Army, came after the Parachute Regiment had completed its own investigations of the weekend's events at Mulligan internment camp, when reporters saw paratroopers club demonstrators and fire rubber bullets at point blank range.

Since the requests were made paratroops have not been used in these sensitive areas of Belfast which are thought to be beginning to calm down. This is because the army believes the absolute minimum of force must be used to prevent the local community from becoming more disaffected with the army.

. . . Undoubtedly the regiment is the one most hated by Catholics in troubled areas, where it has, among local people at least, a reputation for brutality . . . a captain in one regiment whose CO has not made a request said: "They are frankly disliked by many officers here, who regard some of their men as little more than thugs in uniform. I have seen them arrive on the scene, thump up a few people who might be doing nothing more than shouting and jeering . . . they seem to think they can get away with whatever they like."

While Bogside writhed in the depths of agony, new graffiti were to appear on the walls of the Protestant strongholds of the Shankill and Sandy Row in Belfast.

PARAS 13—BOGSIDE 0

WE'VE GOT ONE, WE'VE GOT TWO,
WE'VE GOT THIRTEEN MORE THAN YOU

221

ONE MAN'S BLOODY SUNDAY

Father Edward Daly had been a Bogside priest for ten years. He knew the anti-Internment rally on January 30 would be a large one. There had been talk of ending Internment, but nothing had come of it and it was on everyone's mind. Earlier, he had gone to see one of his parishioners who had been interned. "I didn't recognize him and he didn't recognize me. He was a mumbling fool."

Four years of rioting in Bogside told him that some stone throwing and tussling were to be expected. His routine during a march had been to get down to Bogside to a place called Kells Walk, where a number of elderly people lived on their own. They were particularly frightened of CS gas, and he had evacuated them on numerous occasions.

Before he could leave St. Eugene's Cathedral he had to conduct the late mass. A fellow priest, Father O'Neill, came to him at the altar and whispered that the church was surrounded by paratroopers. He announced it to the congregation and told them to go home quietly. As one of the women passed the soldiers outside he heard her say, "Don't even bother to ignore them."

He changed his vestments and made quickly for the march area. The crowd, as expected, was immense but everything seemed in good humor. As they approached the British blockades on William Street the organizers diverted the rally back to Free Derry Corner.

Some of the younger crowd stayed on and threw stones, which brought a reaction of rubber bullets, water cannon, and some CS gas. He remained at Kells Walk until he figured the rioting was over, leaving his parishioners calm.

At Free Derry Corner he socialized with the milling crowd. A goodly number were about to start home rather than hear the hundredth replay of the Civil Rights record. Bernadette Devlin had been announced as speaker.

"Two shots rang out from a position at the back of the post office sorting office where two paratroopers were stationed. . . . We knew these shots weren't rubber bullets or gas canisters and people just moved away to get near walls. . . . Word came through to me that two people had been shot, a middle-aged man and a teen-aged boy."

He went immediately to the scene on Abbey Street but was informed that they had been taken into a house and a priest was with them.

"The next intimation we got that anything was wrong . . . I must make it perfectly clear, the stoning had completely stopped . . . we heard the sound of heavy engines revving up and I looked over the waste ground toward a place called Sackville Street and saw three or four Saracen armored cars come

dashing in our direction with soldiers on foot behind them. I had experience of this on many occasions before, so I decided to run and get out of the area because it doesn't matter whether you have a Roman collar or a dog collar. . . .

". . . I started running in the general direction of the multistory flats [Rossville] and I had just reached the courtyard. . . . Everybody was running and some people were laughing, there was terrible good humor about it, there was no panic . . . they thought the soldiers would come into the area and stop.

"Suddenly alarm grew when the armored car kept coming on. It suddenly dawned on people that this was something different. I remember a young boy laughing at me. I'm not an athlete and I'm not a very graceful runner. That was the only reason I could think he was laughing. He was very cheery . . . the next thing he suddenly gasped and threw his hands up in the air and fell on his face. I thought he had been hit by a rubber bullet or something and I kept on running because I thought he'd just been knocked off his feet and would get up again."

A huge burst of gunfire opened behind them and the panic was on for fair. Father Daly ducked into a narrow exit blocked by humanity. People tore at a boarded doorway to try to get inside. He spotted a low wall about eighteen inches high and flattened behind it. In retrospect, he recalls having passed it hundreds of times before that day but never seeing it until then.

As the shooting subsided in this period, his mind was on that boy who had fallen, and he maneuvered to a position where he could retrace his steps. The boy was still out there, pitched on his face. The priest left his cover and reached the boy at the same time as a Knight of Malta (Red Cross) aide.

"There was a terrible lot of blood. We pulled up his jersey and there was a massive bloody hole. . . . He asked me, 'Am I going to die?' and I said, 'No,' but I administered last rites. The gunfire started up again and a bullet struck quite close to me. I lay flat beside him and the young Knight of Malta. . . . I remember trying to talk to the wounded lad and calm him. He was getting confused and upset and I can remember him holding my hand and squeezing it. . . . We seemed to be just holding on to one another. The young Knight of Malta lad, who was only sixteen, started to weep. We all wept.

"People from around who were watching got the impression that the soldiers were shooting at us. I just don't know. We were lying flat on our stomachs and the soldiers were just some distance in front of us. There was no one shooting at them, the shooting was coming from them. A fellow about eighteen called Bridge dashed past us shouting, 'Shoot me, shoot me, don't shoot the priest!' and he danced up and down in front of me

Site of the martyrdom of Patrick Joseph Doherty.

THE WIDGERY REPORT: *Age thirty-one . . . his last moments are depicted in a remarkable series of photographs. . . . He was certainly hit from behind whilst crawling or crouching because the bullet entered his buttock and proceeded through his body almost parallel to the spine . . . probability is that he was shot by Soldier F. . . . I conclude that he was not carrying a weapon. . . .*

Father Edward Daly looks down from the Rossville Flats onto the site of the Bloody Sunday massacre.

For a time Father Daly had to leave Derry, for the agony of it had become unbearable. Then, in one of the Hierarchy's most enlightened decisions, he was named Bishop of Derry. This most Christian of men and most gentle of souls has returned to the leper colony of Bogside, for he was incapable of doing less.

223

hysterical . . . he danced out in front of an armored car. . . . I saw a soldier going down on one knee, taking aim, and firing at him. He had two hands up in the air completely hysterical . . . he stumbled and danced crazily around the place and disappeared."

During a lull, some men crawled out and helped get the boy to safety, but as they made their way the fire started up again.

"We got to the top of the street, turned and got the little fellow down. . . . I kneeled beside him and told him, 'Look son, we've got you out.' But he was dead. . . . He was very youthful-looking . . . just in his seventeenth year but only looked about twelve . . . he had a baby face. . . . Jackie Duddy was his name."

THE WIDGERY REPORT: John Francis Duddy. Age 17. According to Mrs. Bonnor he was shot in the back. In fact the bullet entered his right shoulder and travelled through his body from right to left. . . . No shot described by a soldier precisely fits Duddy's case. The nearest is one described by Soldier V who spoke of firing at a man in a white shirt in the act of throwing a petrol bomb, but Duddy was wearing a red shirt and there is no evidence of his having a bomb. . . . I accept that Duddy was not carrying a bomb or firearm.

Father Daly wandered about in a daze and found himself in a house, where a woman gave him tea. He was snapped out of it by an urgent call to the Rossville Flats to a scene of huddled, crouched people and strewn, still bodies.

"One man had the side of his face shot away and he clutched a white handkerchief in his hand. He was a man who went out to try to assist a young boy who was lying groaning and shouting for help. This man took out a white handkerchief and waved it and went out and they shot him. He had seven children. His name was Bernard McGuigan . . . a very good man. . . . I went around and I anointed. . . .

"I think what infuriated everyone was that on the day after that the British Press Office in New York issued that dreadful statement about all of them being gunmen. . . ."

THE WIDGERY REPORT: Bernard McGuigan. Age 41. . . . According to Miss Richmond a wounded man was calling for help and Mr. McGuigan, carrying a white handkerchief, deliberately left a position of cover to attend to him . . . other civilian witnesses confirmed this evidence. . . . I accept her [his wife's] evidence in concluding it is not possible to say that McGuigan was using or carrying a weapon. . . . The paraffin test, however, constitutes ground for suspicion that he had been in close proximity to someone who had fired. . . .

Within the year the commanding officer of 1 Para was knighted for outstanding service to the Crown.

STANLEYS WALK *Outside the former IRA Provo headquarters young people of a new generation ask a centuries-old question.*

5. A DAY ON LOUGH ERNE

The day was so gentle that the lake mirrored itself in a thousand still-life portraits. Set in County Fermanagh and brushing up against the border, Erne runs a course of fifty miles and holds, within, a million pages of history. Scores of inlets and islands bear evidence of pre-Celtic foragers, monastic settlements, Viking battlegrounds and, more recently, the coming of the plantation. Oft visited by pilgrim and warrior, Lough Erne rests now, aloof from the madness around her.

The solitude of that day was punctuated by very little, a passing boat or two, the old canalman cranking the lock gates, a single British helicopter swooping down and passing on.

Three Belfast men, with a Dublin girl in their company, were able to escape the sound and fury for a moment. It was a day of contemplation and lazy exploration. A day the sun chose to shine and was generous with its kisses. For a fleeting time there was peace. Utter, utter peace.

228

Here in the land of the MacGuires the boat glided softly into Castle Archdale Bay, past Strongbow Island, site of a Norman battle, and onto White Island, whose ancient name has been lost.

What a puzzlement was left by the stone carvings and what fraudulent tales have emanated in their wake!

Were they, indeed, the seven deadly sins?

Is the middle figure with hand to mouth really St. Patrick? In County Donegal a carving bearing the same gesture was discovered in the place where "Finn MacCool predicted the birth of Christ." Scholars say the pair to the right of Patrick are the father and son he raised from the dead.

Certainly St. Columba, who visited from Derry, must be among them. Theory abounds on theory. Nearby Boa Island contains a prehistoric graveyard filled with pre-Christian gods.

They mock you and dare you, for within those bland impish faces is locked the cipher of the ages.

I wish I was in Carrickfergus,
Sailing over the deep blue water,
For the seas are deep, love,
And I can't swim over,
And neither or have I wings to fly.
I wish I met with a handy boatman
Who would ferry over my love and I. . . .

DEVENISH-DAMHINIS—The Isle of Oxen

Under St. Molaise, this isle once held one of the greatest monastic scholars, the peer of Columba.

The monks of Devenish were of a reform order known as Culdees, Companions of God. Lough Erne bursts with legend, with its own banshee and ghosts.

Most prominent of the tales is that of the prophet Jeremiah, who fled Jerusalem to be shipwrecked on Ireland's shores, and was found by Finn MacCool. MacCool was taught the ancient Hebrew law of the Torah. Tara, site of the home of the High Kings, allegedly comes from the word "Torah." Jeremiah is said to be buried on Devenish.

6. ALL THE KING'S MEN

The British Army has performed with total consistency in Ireland since the Reformation as an anti-Catholic force of conquest, occupation, colonization, and suppression. This posture has rarely varied.

Deep bonds existed between Protestant Ulster and the army through the Ulster tradition of loyal service and a brilliant array of Ulster officers, including Field Marshals Alexander and Montgomery, in recent times.

The army's affection for Ulster was graphically illustrated by Curragh headquarters in 1912. Ordered north to break up illegal Protestant gunrunning and a secret army, the officers refused. London backed down in face of threatened resignations or possible mutiny.

Since the formation of Northern Ireland, a permanent barracks at Holywood outside Belfast has rotated a token garrison force of some twenty-five hundred men. The Ulster regime was never bashful about calling in more support from the Motherland, and did so in 1922, 1931, 1933, and 1935. Putting the croppies down was established as a standard operation long before the recent troubles broke out.

Today's British Army is in marked contrast to those grand old imperial units and all that blazing ceremonialism. It is a no-nonsense compact, mobile, and mechanized force composed of career professionals and volunteers. Dozens of the traditional regiments have been phased out or kept at token strength, but what remains is probably the best army for its size the British have ever had.

After 1969 the pretense of being an even-handed peace keeper vanished in months, and they were in open warfare against the IRA and titulary, the Catholics. In reversion to historic behavior, both politician and military tread ever so softly on Protestant sensitivities. Midnight raids and Internment had a Catholic monopoly. A fraction of those hauled in under Spe-

A paratrooper patrol slithers along warily in "Apache Country"—Belfast's Bally-murphy District. Maneuvering from cover to cover, the enemy is everywhere, but nowhere to be seen.

cial Powers were Protestant offenders. Largely ignored were secret and illegal Protestant forces far more heavily manned and armed than the IRA.

The Unionist monolith at Stormont ultimately collapsed after Bloody Sunday. Direct rule from London came in the form of the Heath-appointed Supremo, William Whitelaw. He proved a man of infinite patience and fairness in what was one of the most impossible positions in the world. Nonetheless, some of the old attitudes were inbred. Never fully able to grasp Catholic aspirations, he knuckled under to constant Protestant pressure. During his rule Protestant militancy soared without a countercrunch by the army.

Both Whitelaw and the army were to learn that a Catholic could not be suppressed enough to suit an Orangeman. Conversely, any act or action against Protestant extremism brought on condemnations of a "sellout." Nothing would suit these people short of the complete grinding down of the Catholics, and Whitelaw, "their" Supremo, was reviled as, "Whatlaw," "Whitewash" and "outlaw," and their beloved army branded as traitors. Indeed, it was Orangeism's most hysterical moment.

The army's mission became impossibly nightmarish, an epic of frustration. They are bounded by rules well known to IRA and UVF, who took every possible advantage of them. Barricaded in schools, abandoned factories, and the like, they could not set foot into the streets unless on armed patrol. With a Constabulary that had lost its ability to function in large areas, police work fell to an army unsuited for such duty. Hours are exhausting in the cycle of tension-riddled patrols, peace keeping, cordons, car searches, riot control, unending alerts, bomb defusings, snipings, and fire fights. The best they could do was try to hold the lid on the pot and keep it from exploding.

Technique and countertechnique in the bombing war solved one problem just as another was invented. "It's a mind-blowing job. We've got our peckers caught in a revolving door," one colonel remarked. "We're damned if we do and we're damned if we don't. Sure, we can beat guerrilla warfare. It would mean one Bloody Sunday after another, and instead of several hundred internees, we'd lock up thousands. Obviously, this price is too high. We're not a gang of killers. In the face of the abuse we've gotten, I tell you we've shown remarkable restraint."

Relations with the Protestants are now icy. After the dangers of the street, the British stay pinned in their barracks, doomed to eternal boredom. Four months of Ulster duty is about all a man can take before his unit is rotated out. Even if Bloody Sunday, Internment, the interrogations, and some of the more prominent incidents had never occurred, there was never any way for the army to win a popularity contest in Ulster.

The experience has created disenchantment. Many officers and men came over zealously believing in Ulster's right as a

British province. The general consensus now is a longing to "get the hell out and let the bloody Irish solve their own affairs."

Disengagement is not possible. Britain's debt is not settled. There is no way the British could continue as a respected people after a desertion that would bring on a civil war. Carnage after a British Army withdrawal is too horrible to comprehend. In this sense they are a peace force staving off a blood bath until the politicians can establish an order with which both sides will live.

Constructed in recent years, a grim jerry-built public-housing estate in Ballymurphy has become derelict. Its people plagued by unemployment, the stenches of poverty are everywhere. Paving stones have been jerked up as missiles, street lighting ripped off as fusing switches for bombs, broken glass unswept; filth and graffiti perpetuate hate and spawn the next generation's revolutionaries. As the Para patrol hangs close to the walls, the only sign of elegance is the Catholic church at the foot of the street.

Belfast schools have become choice locations for barrack-fortresses. They are always centrally 'set in a neighborhood, and cooking and toilet facilities are readily available. Classrooms are converted into barracks, and the three- and four-storied rooftops make excellent observation posts.

When an army presence is established in the middle of a Catholic neighborhood, a continual round of patrols is maintained to keep the area off balance. The presence of troops in the daytime is announced by clanging noises and at night by flicking lights off and on.

The atmosphere on both sides of the hastily built corrugated walls is supercharged with fear and loathing.

On the theory that half a school is better than none, sandbags in mid-corridor mark the dividing line. A public relations campaign and good will gestures in Protestant schools have made this situation bearable.

In Catholic schools the armor is heavier, the weapons at alert, and feeling between soldier and child one of consuming tension. Classrooms are jammed beyond capacity, giving credence to the argument that it is impossible to educate a child under such conditions.

236

Strategic deployment has brought into being a variety of operational bases and living quarters. In downtown Belfast a large unit is housed in the heart of the most troubled area. Screened off by wire fencing, the passage becomes extremely difficult for the would-be bomber. Such places may no longer be safe or viable because of recent **IRA** introduction of more sophisticated weaponry, including rockets and mortars.

EAGLE PATROL

In the countryside the troops are stretched more thinly, with greater areas to cover, and the roads bristle with traps. Tens of dozens of border crossings make it impossible to adequately cover the notorious smuggling thoroughfares.

As a counter strike force, the eagle patrol was created. A squad of men leap from their helicopter at road X, Y, or Z. The craft becomes airborne in seconds and flies from view. Ducking behind the omnipresent stone walls, the troops jump out suddenly and block an unsuspecting vehicle. If the search turns up something suspicious, they are in immediate radio contact for intelligence information.

It is a game of averages, which must be played in a never ending search for new chess moves.

Dawn Patrol on the border in a Republican hotspot.

LLOYD GEORGE'S FOLLY

The mad border that runs its hundred-and-fifty-mile course from Derry to Warrenpoint presents a logistical backbreaker. Most of the border area is in hill farms, a poor variety of land worked by Ulster's Catholics. The border is a traditional Republican hotbed. Free passage back and forth has been unalterably established by two generations of smugglers and gunrunners. Once across into the Republic, a man on the run has established semi-sanctuary.

Napoleon realized the impossibility of containing smuggling, even in a small area. The Germans in World War II found they were unable to prevent it in the tight confines of the few square miles of the Warsaw ghetto.

Even with the complete co-operation of Republic forces, which they do not have nor ever will get, the British could not seal the border with a hundred thousand troops.

The army is not allowed to engage in a battle of attrition. Executions and village burnings of the Black and Tan days have given way to a more civilized stance of low profile. Intelligence information is hard to come by. Out here, informers are a scarce commodity. The rules state the British can pursue only up to the border, but they may not cross it.

The best they can hope for is to get a fair share with the options of eagle patrols, mobile strikes, roadblocks, and painfully pieced intelligence.

In places such as Crossmaglen, the troops are buttoned up even tighter than they are in the cities. The roads have proved to be death traps. Quick and inexperienced answering of an alarm could well mean walking into a land mine. Patrols are forced to clear the way painstakingly on foot before armor can follow.

The IRA uses the border in much the same way that a ringwise fighter plays off the ropes. Roads are mined on the Ulster side, but wires and detonation switches are in the Republic.

Troops out here in "Apache Country" are truly isolated outposts, for life outside the barrack/fort is nonexistent. For their entire four-month tour, they are likely not to receive a single friendly greeting. At the end of the tour even the strongest nerves are frayed.

Gordon Highlanders, Fusiliers, Anglians, Coldstreams, yes, and even the Paras . . . all the king's men know the damnable futility of grasping mercury and watching it slip through their fingers.

A façade of business as usual ironically continues.

7. MAY GOD HAVE MERCY ON BELFAST

A turn-of-the-century Victorian edifice, the Belfast City Hall remains a staunch sym-bol of Ulster's determination to retain her British connection. The scene of the sign-ing of the Act of Covenant in 1912 and home of Northern Ireland's first Parliament, it stands unscathed in the middle of the bomb-racked commercial center of Belfast.

The Celtic word "Belfast" means "approach to the sand spit." Until 1600 there wasn't much there but a wide spot in the river. An early member of the Chichester family staked claim to it after the "Flight of the Earls" and received a charter for a family borough. Belfast and surrounding Counties Down and Antrim are the true heartland of the Presbyterian settlement.

For the first hundred years the community toddled along, establishing a middling trading and commercial town. In addition to the Presbyterian qualities of piety and hard work, the originals from Scotland were liberal and enlightened. They, too, had come under persecution from many of the Penal Laws, and a great number emigrated to America in the eighteenth-century Scotch-Irish exodus.

Theobald Wolfe Tone found the atmosphere so rich that the United Irishmen was born in Belfast. When the first Catholic church was established at the end of the eighteenth century, an openhearted Presbyterian community greeted it with brotherly love.

Her situation at the geographical center of Presbyterian Down and Antrim, on a natural body of navigable water, caused Belfast to extend her boundaries continually in monotonous red brick clusters.

Nearly all of the early population came in from surrounding farm lands, where communal living and work sharing were traditional. The togetherness of the agrarian society was continued in Belfast. People banded together in subcommunities, giving the town more an appearance of little linked-up villages than that of an urban center.

The open-minded character of the people faded during the Wolfe Tone Uprising of 1798. Belfast itself was reasonably placid, but out on the land the division between Catholic and Protestant had opened and then split into a permanent scar with the formation of the Orange Order.

By 1800, Belfast had entered the Industrial Revolution, a half century late. An enormous textile complex brought with it the vilest slums in the British Isles. Agricultural landlordism found its urban counterpart in the creation of a raw, ugly monstrosity. The Marquess of Donegal became one of the largest rent collectors in the realm, squandering his fortune into bankruptcy through gambling, and letting the ill-conceived housing fall further into squalor.

The stink of Belfast's poor districts flowed in open sewers and erupted from piles of uncollected dunghills; it was intermixed with the odors of home breweries, tanneries, and ammoniated urine on walls and gutters. The defilement was locked inside tight little courtyarded dwellings, and air and light were locked out. Families numbering a dozen or more huddled in single-room hovels without water or sanitation. The few public bathhouses could not cope with the crush of filth. Open

sores, matted hair, warped growth, and sunken-eyed madness were the dress of the people.

The looms boomed on relentlessly, first cotton, then linen. The more delicate linen work required women and children. The latter were supplied by overcrowded orphanages. Belfast, like Derry, became a city of female labor toiling in unspeakably dingy, unsafe factories.

For Belfast's first two hundred years, there was no significant Catholic population. They drifted in, in the wake of evictions and perennial unemployment, and the trickle became a flood during and after the famine. Like the Presbyterians, they settled in their own small communities around the heartbeat of a church. Neither welcome nor wanted, they came into an established order in which they shared no involvement. Job competition was already fierce, and the massive Catholic influx terrified the Protestant workers like nothing else. Catholic villages linked up in the western part of the city. In other areas Catholics lived in surrounded enclaves such as Ardoyne, New Lodge, and Short Strand. What were once communal settlements became tribal areas of two hostile clans.

Industry exploded for fair with the arrival of the power loom. About the girth of Lough Belfast and in towns to the south, hundreds of looms sprang up along avenues of running water. With the collapse of cotton during the American Civil War, Belfast became the linen capital of the world.

In 1859 the Harland and Wolff shipyard opened to become the very power base of Belfast's industrial might. For the first time thousands of males were put to work . . . but nearly to a man they were Protestant. The Belfast complex multiplied into heavy machinery, armaments, ropemaking, distilling, tobacco, flour, graving docks, and a major port.

Nothing would ever again keep the pall of smoke from inundating Belfast. By 1870, commissions of inquiry expressed deep concern over air and water pollution. This was causing debilitation of workers, particularly in jobs like hackling linen, and a fair part of the work force kept going on alcohol and dope.

Protestant slums and the waterfront were desperate with crime and inhumanity. Catholic slums were the worst cesspools in the British Isles, and neither law nor even clergy cared to visit. They were frequent hosts to onslaughts of cholera and typhoid, with an incidence of TB double that of the rest of Britain. Beggars, fever carts, workhouses, prostitution, killings, all in a haze of alcohol, were workaday. When there was no dog- or cockfight to wager on, mothers threw their sons into the pit to battle themselves bloody for a penny or two.

Outside the ghettos, great blocklike, uninspired Victorian edifices created a contrast of elegance with putridity, grandeur of empire with swill. As buildings for commerce, industry, and government rose in the center, a necklace of manor houses

hugged the sea in the world's newest gold coast.

The "Golden Age of Riots" entered to the sound of the damnations of fire-breathing evangelists who kept the Protestant poor on knife's edge. Mammoth open-air meetings by the Rev. Messrs. Drew, Cooke, Hanna, and their ilk burst into savage sectarian rioting in 1813, 1832, 1835, 1852, 1864, 1872, 1880, 1884, 1886, and 1898. Commissions of inquiry just couldn't figure out what was the matter. Post-World War I riots against Catholics raged in the early 1920s and into the depression years. This "Lord's work" has been valiantly carried on by the Ian Paisleys with unrelenting fury, directly up to the recent holocaust.

It has always been the poor harangued to fight the poor, the tribal units of Protestants in Sandy Row, Shankill, and East Belfast pitted against Catholic tribes in the Falls and Andersontown.

When Belfast was granted city status in 1888 the structure of rule was firmly implanted. The gentry had gained control of the Unionist Party with the interlocked power of the Orange Order and a segment of rabble-rousing clergy. Police and government apparatus were solidly in their hands. Belfast was divided into fifteen wards, two of them going to the Catholics with twenty-five per cent of the population.

By the twentieth century Belfast was a major spoke in the British scheme of things, a manufacturing giant with a windfall for the elite and prosperity for many. For the poor, Protestant loyalty was rewarded by jobs. It was Ulsterism at its grossest level, a society existing by committing economic homicide on the native. The good life here and all things from it were tied to the benefits of being a British city, and any talk of Irish rule or a split from the Motherland brought a reaction of frenzy.

This skillful separation of the working classes has always been the principal canon of Ulsterism. The deplorable housing continues on. Outdoor privies abound. Progress for the workingman is replaced by threats of unemployment. Liberal thought is drenched under Orange nonsense and holy-rolling muckraking. In the end the Protestant worker has been bilked. He, too, has been kept on the edge of squalor, and his diet of medieval meanderings is all he has to hang on to. He continues to live a breath away from a riot.

Belfast was put into business for a certain purpose, and she operated in a certain manner. She is the mongoloid child born out of British imperialism, the water and oil that would never mix, and a blight on the human spirit.

247

Red brick in the city,
White horse on the wall,
Italian marble in the City Hall,
O stranger from England,
Why stand so aghast?
May the Lord in His mercy
Be kind to Belfast.

This city that houses
Our hopes and our fears
Was knocked up from the swamp
In the last hundred years.
But the last shall be first,
And the first shall be last.
May the Lord in His mercy
Be kind to Belfast.

We swore by King William,
There'd never be seen,
An all Irish Parliament
At College Green
So at Stormont we're nailing
Our flag to the mast.
May the Lord in His Mercy,
Be kind to Belfast.

The bricks they will mourn
And the stones they will weep,
And the damp Lagan fog
Lull the city to sleep.
It's to hell with the future,
And live in the past.
May the Lord in His mercy
***Be kind** to Belfast.*
Maurice James Craig

DIVIS (above) *Like her nearby sister Unity Flats, and Rossville in Derry, instant vertical slums have replaced century-old Catholic ghettos, becoming battlegrounds and IRA strongholds. Divis' proximity to Protestant Shankill keeps a specter of rioting always at hand.*

HARLAND AND WOLFF

H&W is Ulster's greatest single industrial complex. For more than a century it has been a major force in world shipbuilding and marine engineering. The Queen's Island Yard, striding the mouth of the river Lagan as it flows into Belfast Lough, holds Britain's largest facility. The new drydock is capable of building a pair of quarter-million-tonners simultaneously.

The Goliath crane, an engineering masterpiece, stands visible for all of Belfast to see as symbol of the industrial might of the province.

Goliath first broke into the skyline in 1969, the vintage year of Civil Rights and riots. Although H&W's canned history reads like a Who's Who in the progress of ships, it is incredibly devoid of mention of the problems of a mixed workforce of Protestants and Catholics.

In the present era the working force is in the neighborhood of ten thousand men. Depending on who is telling the story, there are a few dozen to a few hundred Catholics. Certain explanations seem valid enough. In the beginning skilled ship building workers immigrated from Scotland seeking employ-

ment. The system of family purchase of apprenticeships insured this continuity. Not to be overlooked is the tribal make-up of Belfast and a long-standing marriage between East Belfast and H&W.

Nevertheless the Protestant workers maintain the practice of Ulsterism. One has only to walk through the yard during the marching season to get a clear-cut picture of God, King, and Ulster.

H&W argue that the composition of the workforce was not of their making. Nonetheless, until the end of the 1960s they did not check the practice of Ulsterism by the majority of their employees.

A new and enlightened management recognizes openly for the first time that labor relations are the major problem. But Ulsterism demands that there be no change in the status quo, the Protestant workers are entrenched, and any whiff of a Catholic intrusion in the yard will sound a war cry. In the end they will give "Not an Inch," and there will be "No Surrender." After all, that is what their Ulster is all about.

WILLIAM CRAIG

William Craig is not so eloquent in his anti-Nationalist diatribes as his fellow Protestant Ian Paisley. Nonetheless it would be well not to underestimate the political influence of the man. He was sacked as Minister of Home Affairs by Prime Minister Terence O'Neill in 1968 after disagreements about reform. He climbed to a leading position in the Protestant system as the hardest of the hard-liners and became the leader of both the paramilitary vanguard movement and the ultra-right-wing vanguard party, both dedicated to a policy of not yielding an inch.

Craig was widely looked to as a future Unionist leader, especially in the aftermath of the Ulster Workers' strike of 1974, which destroyed Brian Faulkner's power-sharing coalition. But more recently Craig has made an interesting effort to break the deadlock that has since existed. Perhaps more interested in power than in his diehard principles, he seems to be trying to lead the Unionist Party out of a cul-de-sac secession and toward more limited—if temporary—accommodation with the Catholics.

Certainly Craig's record and past utterances do not suggest that he is a compromiser or libertarian, and the Catholic population has no reason to love or trust him on his record. But he is the only Unionist of any stature who, since spring 1974, has been able to offer his party any alternative to complete intransigeance.

GO
SLOW
UDA CHECKPOINT

GENTLEMEN OF THE ULSTER DEFENSE
ASSOCIATION

An embattled Protestant neighborhood locks itself in with a neighborhood defense force. The UDA is borderline in legality and considers it safer to work in the open than be driven underground. The largest of the militant organizations, it numbers tens of thousands of workingmen, mostly in tense urban areas. The inner councils have been torn apart by strife and gang-land-like assassinations of their own leadership. Terrified of a British sellout and no longer trusting their own politicians, they personify the abandoned orphans of Britain. They know now that their fervent love of the Crown is not returned. It is the split personality of the Ulsterman, who, in his quandary, may tragically turn to Smyth, Paisley, and Craig.

SANDY ROW

THE GLORIOUS TWELFTH

THE SHANKILL

SNIPER'S ALLEY *In the Catholic enclave of The Markets, a litter of brickbats hurled at the British armored patrol fills the street. Once a dwelling is abandoned, the windows are bricked up to deny sniper positions and to stop homeless families from squatting. A woman with a carriage keeps a cautious eye out. There may be more than children playing at the end of the lane.*

GUNFIGHT ON THE PEACE LINE *Along the Crumlin Road "peace line" a gunfight breaks out with firing from the tormented Catholic enclave of Ardoyne.*

8. THE VICTIMS

IS THERE A LIFE BEFORE DEATH?

The ugliness of sectarian warfare has revolted and shocked the unshockable. Bodies blown apart by the bomber are swept up into plastic bags before television audiences. The daily torture, mutilation, and dismemberment preceding the execution are detailed in the *Telegraph*.

People slowly brink toward madness as the shooting goes on night after night, bullets whining and pocking off the plaster. The bomb lights the sky and rumbles the earth and shatters the ear. All one can beg for is a single night's sleep.

The day of the IRA bomber has escalated into the Protestant murder squad. Sectarian killers kill for the sake of killing. Murder is done before the eyes of the children . . . the man had seven children. . . . A girl and a boy in a parked car shot through the head . . . a child's hands blown off by a booby trap . . . a woman blinded by a rubber bullet . . . Murder . . . murder . . . murder . . . Protestant . . . Catholic . . . Catholic . . . Protestant . . . it doesn't matter any more, as murder is avenged by murder. The IRA is through, says the weekly British press release. A building is devastated in answer. There is no beginning or end any more.

It's so safe to kill. No one will turn anyone in. There is no law . . . no compassion . . . it's all collapsed . . . sit and pray from the time the child goes off to school until you hear his steps return . . . or will it be his steps?

OH GOD! screams out a tortured writing on the wall. . . . IS THERE A LIFE BEFORE DEATH?

THE AGONY OF THE CHRIST CHILD
From a sculpture by Dr. Con McCluskey

260

FATHER EDWARD DALY WITH PARISHIONERS

The television blared but no one was listening. There is such an aura of hurt about Catherine Gilmore that one cannot talk too long to her about it. She looks at you, but she just isn't there. Henry Gilmore shakes his head. "It was just a peaceful gathering. Everyone seemed so happy that day."

Now it's like living in a graveyard. Derry's Rossville is in the middle of all that death. Nothing is the same. Sadie Moore upstairs won't go outside again. Groceries, everything, are brought in to her. All she pleads for is one single night's sleep.

Catherine and Henry Gilmore were fairly typical Bogsiders. Two of their eight children died very young of disease. After years of waiting they were able to obtain a tiny apartment in the Rossville Flats. On that terrible Sunday she watched the parade from her balcony. She witnessed Jack Duddy being struck down and the turmoil that ensued.

Out of her back window she was able to make out a body. She could not identify it . . . a pair of feet and a hump. An hour after the firing, she was told that the body was her youngest son Hugh's.

THE WIDGERY REPORT: HUGH PIUS GILMORE, AGE 17 . . . According to Miss Richmond he was one of a crowd of 30 to 50 people who ran away down Rossville Street when the soldiers appeared. . . . Gilmore was shot by one of the soldiers who fired from Kells Walk . . . it is impossible to identify the soldier. Gilmore's reaction to paraffin test was negative. There is no evidence that he used a weapon.

MAN IN THE MIDDLE

The Rev. Joseph Parker was chief chaplain of the Flying Angel Club, a seamen's mission near the waterfront on Corporation Street. It was part of a world-wide group of church-operated homes away from home for visiting sailors. Sometimes the activities were printed in ten languages. Since the troubles began, it had been increasingly difficult to get girls to come out at night and serve as hostesses. Early in 1972 part of the building was done in by a nearby bomb.

In his modest home in a middle-class neighborhood, Joe Parker was family man to his wife Dorothy and their three children. One good thing about being in Tokyo Gardens, it was far from the bombing runs and a decent place to raise his brood.

What deeply disturbed the Rev. Mr. Parker also deeply disturbed his neighbors and that "silent majority," both Catholic and Protestant. These were the folks in the middle, trapped between extreme elements and without a cohesive voice to speak for them. They were all reasonable people, educated, settled, positioned. They knew how to give and take love and were open to any fair solution to stop the mayhem. But the man in the middle is generally fragmented because he is not a joiner of the mob. It takes so very long for him to become aroused, and it is so difficult for him to be heard.

Joe Parker is a true servant of God. He sought Christian answers to the crushing events, but his voice of moderation was too often drowned by the roar of the demagogue. Nonetheless, like any decent human being, he was deeply and broodingly concerned.

The youngest of the Parker children was fourteen-year-old Stephen. The boy always wore a smile on his face because he was never taught to hate. He was a member of the Belfast Youth Orchestra, and the music they played together was harmony, not discord. The day was Friday, July 21, 1972. Stephen was ready to make off for the shopping center on Cavehill Road, where he did weekend deliveries for pocket money. He told his mum he had a premonition of something bad. She smiled it off. Their neighborhood was really quite safe . . . the dreadful times put such ideas into his head.

At 2:09 P.M. a bomb went off across town in the Lisburn Road area. At two thirty-six another bomb destroyed a small hotel. Well, that wasn't so unusual for any ordinary Friday in Belfast these days. But this was no ordinary Friday.

At two-forty a branch of the Ulster Bank was bombed, and in the next hour eight more bombs exploded. At three-ten the Oxford Street bus station was destroyed without warning, and six people were killed.

Pandemonium . . . total confusion and hysteria were breaking out all over Belfast. People ran away from one bomb and around the corner into another. They scurried in screaming antlike circles, certain the world was coming to an end.

At three-twenty a car bomb exploded in the Cavehill Shopping Center.

"When I got to the mortuary I knew there was a boy, the body of a boy there. I looked immediately for someone with fair hair. I was somewhat relieved that the hair was dark, but, of course, it was singed and burnt dark with the heat of the explosion. I thought immediately, though: it's not Stephen. And then I looked quickly again. I recognized the shirt as similar to the one Stephen had been wearing, but again it had been affected by the explosion. The belt was a Scout belt: he was a Scout, and a few days ago he put these studs all round in the belt and he stood there getting me to admire them; he was very clothes conscious. I asked one of the men: would he look in the pockets. I wanted to be absolutely sure. Anyway, he looked in the pockets and found this box of matches—trick matches that Stephen had used that evening before to fool me. And I saw they had no proper maker's label. But I wanted to be sure again—you cling onto everything—so I asked if anybody had a box of safety matches so I could strike one. The police were wonderful; they found somebody in the road and they came in. I struck one, and then I tried it on the other. Then I knew it was Stephen."

(AUG 1971)
STEPHEN PARK

Before this day was done, twenty-two bombs had exploded within ninety minutes. Eleven people had been blown to death and a hundred and thirty more wounded and injured. The IRA lost the hearts of many of their own people and much of the human race.

There is something Godlike about Joe Parker and his wife that keeps them from being consumed with bitterness. His most fervent prayers are for the power to forgive, and he says it will not have been in vain if a new Ireland can come from it. He takes upon himself his share of society's responsibility for those who perpetrated the blood orgy. He has staged hunger strikes in protest against the moral and political bankruptcy. With all this courage he cannot conceal the pangs of everlasting agony, and as he pleads with you for peace, there is a haunting look in his eyes and he repeats over and over: "You know what I mean, don't you? You know what I mean?"

THEY WON'T COME HOME AGAIN

What with the passing of jobs and sashes and the close neighborhoods and communal tradition, the Belfast family can be unusually tight knit. Such a family were Francis and Joan Orr and their three sons. Their small row house on Alliance Road, which touched up against Catholic Ardoyne, was a shade better than most. The Orrs were a bit different, in that they had nothing to do with politics, marching, or rioting. Malcolm, the oldest at twenty, was the only Protestant working for a Catholic construction firm in Andersontown and was engaged to marry a Catholic girl.

He was extremely shy when they met. Malcolm didn't drink, smoke, gamble, or use foul language. He had been made to feel like a son in her parents' home, a compliment which the Orrs returned her in full measure. Pete, the middle son at nineteen, was completely taken by them too. The younger son, David, at seventeen was not quite buddying around with his brothers yet.

"The last night we saw each other," Malcolm's fiancée said, "we talked about going away. If we were to set up a home, we didn't want to do it here, because things had really gotten that bad. There was no longer any point in staying in Ireland. It was Malcolm's mother and father and my parents who wanted us, you know, but he thought it would be better for us to go. We had to consider their feelings because the Orrs were the most wonderful family in the world."

Pete and Malcolm left one evening for her home. She was expecting them, and when they didn't arrive she phoned the Orrs. In Belfast an instant reaction of fear can be anticipated. Francis and Joan Orr set out to check other possible places the boys might have gone and, not finding them, reported to the police, then sat close to the television to hear the news. Ten to seven . . . ten to eight . . . nine o'clock. Between nine and ten there was nothing to report.

"We thought someone had kidnaped them and given them

a hiding or something like that," Francis said. "I told the police I hoped they were found in a hospital just knocked down by a car. . . . At half past eleven there was a news flash . . . two bodies had been found and I knew . . . in my heart . . . I knew it was my two sons"

Joan Orr fortified herself. A Belfast mother learns to do that. "My boys have no sin to answer for," Joan said. "They were very good to me . . . always giving me little gifts and we joked about a great deal. I just lived for them, which I think maybe has been my punishment. I thought too much of my own little family and not enough of the world outside of me. . . . My husband and I didn't believe in this terrible division in religion that exists in Ireland. . . . They welcomed my son into their home. They couldn't have been any kinder to him, and the same with Peter's friend. We didn't object because Peter's friend was a Catholic boy, because John is a very good boy, and if Peter was with Johnny, we knew he was in good company.

"This last couple of years Malcom's world was surrounded by his girl friend. She was a very sweet little girl . . . but other than that, he loved to go fishing, and of course he had been steadily attending the technical college in his trade . . . Peter? Peter loved to tinker around with old cars and the usual football and pop music . . . just ordinary boys . . . attended their work very well. . . ."

The bodies of Malcolm and Peter Orr were found dumped in a lane outside Belfast. They had been executed and lay face down in tall grass atop one another.

During the era of tragedy Joan Orr had felt deeply over every casualty but didn't really know what it was like till then. There was an outpouring of sympathy from Catholic and Protestant alike, in this tragic replay of the Romeo and Juliet theme. The most moving gesture of all came from the parents of two young Scottish Fusiliers who had been similarly shot in the back of the head and dumped in the execution that hastened the end of the Chichester-Clark regime.

Francis Orr had known only hard work and family. To the day their sons died, his wife was at her factory job. He feels that there is no need of vengeance and even pities his sons' killers, for he knows that here or elsewhere they will have that moment of facing their Maker.

The room was very simple, as their life had been. They didn't photograph much . . . just a couple of old pictures that didn't do the boys much justice. Young David entered the house, tried to force a smile, and retreated upstairs. She looked after him. . . . "I used to think if anything happened to my sons I would know real hatred, but it leaves you so empty to think somebody else would die for killing your son. It doesn't bring your son back. Revenge is empty. . . . I feel sorry for them,

for they are getting their punishment" Her mind drifted. . . . "People should be allowed to pick their own friends without interference from outsiders." She blinked listlessly and whispered, "I hope somebody will show me how to live again, because I don't feel as if I want to.

"I just couldn't think that my sons were never going to walk into my house again. At times I never want to leave my house because I can walk into their bedrooms and feel near to them. I never want to leave Ireland because I couldn't bear to feel I'd be leaving them. . . . Sometimes I can go about my work and again, at the times they would be coming in at night and the times they would be getting up in the morning, I just don't know how I get through those times because that's when it hits me the hardest. . . . Oh yes, I go into their rooms. I still say good night to them and God bless. . . .

". . . I felt like running out into the middle of the road and shouting, 'For God's sake, stop it . . . it's senseless.' . . . I don't know any gunman but if I could get through to his mind . . . The suffering that is going on in this place . . . it's like sitting back and watching a nation committing suicide and there's not a thing you can do about it. . . . You don't want others to go through the desolation you are going through. . . . I wouldn't want anybody else to have it. . . . Yesterday I was out and there were two little boys fighting in the street. I ran over and picked one up and said to the other, 'Don't hurt him.' . . . I can't bear to see anybody hurting another human being now."

Francis Orr had heard that two Catholic boys had been executed. His prayer has been constant that no revenge killing should take place for Peter and Malcolm. It would be the last thing his sons would have wanted.

"I want the people of England to bear with us a while longer and try to understand that we want to get the same life as they have in Oxford, Manchester, Cambridgeshire, Yorkshire, Lancashire, Surrey, and Devon. If we could have the same life . . . perhaps . . . perhaps if their troops could stay a little while longer . . . their sons . . . I pray for them at night . . . I hope the soldiers don't die. . . . I hate to hear guns firing . . . every night I lie in bed and listen to fifty shots, a hundred shots, and I wonder. . . . It's depressing . . . so very depressing."

They put off the funeral for as long as possible. They sat by the coffins and spoke to each other and their boys. And then it could no longer be delayed. He walked between their coffins, one hand resting on each son all the way to the cemetery. The house had been filled. She was there with her family and many other Catholic families. Protestants were there and many, many strangers and they prayed together.

For a passing moment there was a family of man in Ulster.

9. FRIDAY'S CHILDREN

Friday's child is full of woe,
Saturday's child has far to go. . . .

CHILD'S PLAY

"It's a sixer!" shouts the lookout. With those words begins a favorite Belfast children's game. Rocks in hands, they edge out to the street. Some of them couldn't be older than five or six. The six-wheeled British Saracen armored vehicle probes its way knowingly toward an intersection in the gut center of the Catholic Falls district. The children howl about it like a pack of avenging wolves, and the missiles staccato off the iron skin. Inside, the noise is deafening. Buckets of paint have been slung over it in an attempt to blot out vision through the periscope. For a time they tried to clean the vehicles daily, but now they wait till they're rotated out of Ulster.

In the photograph below left, taken through a viewing slit inside the Saracen, a boy cranks up to let one go. The aim can be deadly. On one occasion a driver was hit and the car overturned, killing several soldiers locked inside. The boy who threw it became a neighborhood hero.

They are children, but they reflect their parents' hatred of the British. When such madness is tolerated as normal behavior, prospects for the future seem chilling.

WITHOUT WARNING

The atmosphere was supercharged in Belfast's Lenadoon Estate. The army claimed there was unusual IRA activity and that they were coming under unduly heavy fire. The residents counterclaimed that the army wanted an excuse to set up observation posts on the high buildings which would put them under siege.

It was turning evening. Things were settling down for the late meal. Two of the kids were taking a bath and two others were at the kitchen table.

The quiet was punctured by a fusillade of bullets ripping into the top story of one of the blocks. Casualties were missed by a miraculous hair, but a terrified evacuation followed by those families facing the army posts. They returned because there was no place else to go, and they live in the cross hairs of a gun sight.

It's difficult to sleep now. The children are frightened, and no one can tell when it will happen again without warning.

"My Daddy is dead four weeks now, and that's a month. He died on Wednesday morning at half six. He was beaten up in August because he tried to stop them from burning the houses in our street. He was in the hospital four weeks before he died. My Daddy said to me when he was living, he said, 'you'll grow up, you'll be a man like me.' He said because I bring dogs and cats into the house and so did he. He brought home fish and all.

"My Mommy said he died happy because he died in his sleep. When the smoke started coming from the walls of our house, we ran out and down the entry. My budgie and frogs and my cat and hampster were burned in the house. This is the second time we were burned out.

"When the slates were cracking with the heat, we thought it was guns and we cut over into another entry and went to our Granny's house.

"My aunt gave me a dog. I call it Arco. I have a wishing well and I save up money in it. When I have three shillings, I'll buy a goldfish."

Letter from a Belfast child

They live in Short Strand, the most vulnerable and isolated Catholic enclave in Belfast. On this day an Orange parade passed. The army had erected a high canvas wall so that neither side could catch sight of the other. By some strange quirk, these little girls in Sunday best were not frightened. On the other hand, the soldier was rather young and his smile was warm and could hardly be resisted.

BELFAST PLAYGROUNDS — PROTESTANT

BELFAST PLAYGROUNDS — CATHOLIC

Protestant Shankill

Catholic Falls

CONCLUSION

The old order is dead. Ulsterism can no longer function in the six counties of Northern Ireland. For the half century it held power, the Unionist Party had embodied every facet of Protestant thinking. After the fall of Stormont, the Unionists segmented into numerous splinter groups. The Orange Order no longer controls the party executive and is, itself, on the defensive.

After the convulsion of internment and direct rule from London, followed by years of bombings and sectarian madness, there was a brief trend toward reasonableness. Brian Faulkner, indeed, seemed to be dancing on the head of a pin. It was not that he and his colleagues were suddenly smitten with liberalism; they were expedient men sharp enough to realize their particular totalitarian epoch was over.

A new power-sharing structure was hammered out, based on proportional representation and a small measure of co-operation with the Republic. For the first time, Catholics were to have a stake in running the province. Former bitter political enemies were now sitting and talking to each other. Men previously considered radical and dangerous were part of the new executive. It was progress and there seemed to be light at the end of a three-hundred-and-fifty-year tunnel.

But at the same time, the extreme elements on both sides polarized even more rigidly. Ian Paisley and William Craig, whose stars had seemed eclipsed, were suddenly more powerful than ever, dedicated to the destruction of any scheme for sharing power with the Catholics. "Not an inch" was no archaic remembrance but yet another new chapter of the Reformation. The old bromides were hauled out and ancient fears invoked. The rhetoric dripped with venom. "British treachery is shoving the loyalists into a union with the Republic" This tactic never failed to work in the past and now was no exception.

Craig and Paisley represent a militant crowd, certainly strong enough to impose total havoc. Moderates and liberals were swept out of office in the ensuing election, to be replaced by dogmatic hard liners. This was followed by a general strike that ultimately brought down the short-lived power-sharing executive.

The air has become alive with the threat to declare Ulster's independence. If such a thing were to happen, any new state created by the Paisley/Craig faction would assure continuation of hell on earth for the Catholics and would more than likely plunge Ulster into a barbaric civil war.

A very real fear is that a Paisley/Craig-run Ulster would be followed by a bloody pogrom against the Catholics. Such a pogrom would almost certainly force an armed response from the Republic. With the British Army no longer around, it is academic to conclude what would follow.

An independent Ulster, with or without civil war, would be an economic catastrophe. Survival without the British connection is a moot point. Yet, with all the danger it implies, talk of independence persists, for there simply is not enough charity or justice to create anything other than a monster regime. It must be remembered that Craig and Paisley speak for the will of the majority of the Protestants.

At the other end of the spectrum, the IRA had its own role in destroying the power-sharing executive. The IRA knows it cannot win militarily and there is no way it can force a million Protestants to capitulate to its unconditional demands. Those brilliant minds of the 1916 Easter Rising are long gone. Today's IRA will not face political exposure by placing itself before the voter. To do so would reveal its glaring political ineptness and the lack of public support for its ideas.

If there is a way to defeat the IRA, it is by giving justice to the Catholics. A man with a good job, living in a decent home, with a promise of a future, is not so likely to want to give up his evening to manufacture and plant bombs. But the lack of jobs is the bane of Ulster's existence; justice for Catholics is what the conflict is all about and the farthest thing from the minds of Ian Paisley and William Craig. The IRA can be depended upon to continue to flourish in the putridity of the ghettos. So long as it flourishes it will justify its existence by lofty and unrealistic revolutionary visions. It will never have the might to do what it says it must, but it will never be able to leave its people to the "tender mercy" of the jackals.

From the British view, Ulster is no longer an asset, but a liability to the British taxpayer. The British Army has knuckled under in the face of rising Protestant militancy and has only been partly effective against the IRA. England is painfully aware that it has been hoodwinked by a half century of Unionist intimidation and manipulation and has paid for much of Ulster's prosperity out of its own pocket.

The British would love dearly to see the Protestants of Ulster become Irishmen and "let the Irish settle their own affairs." The Crown which once gloried in Ulster's ultra-loyalty is now apt to be embarrassed by it. The British know that the loyalty was lavished by the Ulsterman as a method of paying his dues and buying cheap insurance. They know that the Ulster love of the Crown had the biggest Catch-22 of them all: the proposition that Britain was going to be used to allow their quasi-fascist regime to exist.

The question is how to disengage. The British are paying the final, awful price for imperial adventure. What would happen in the eyes of the world if England pulled out and left Ulster to a holocaust? For the sake of face, England must continue to play out the unwanted role of a nation ostensibly protecting one of its provinces. In reality, she wishes nothing more desperately than to pack up and leave. The British public is getting fed up and vocal. The fall of the power-sharing coalition was a body blow to hopes of a peaceful solution.

The Northern Irish Catholic has suffered a terrible disenchantment. All those mountains of Republican prose he had been weaned on proved to be so much hot air when he was in trouble. For fifty years, it would have meant political suicide in the Republic not to pay lip service to reunification. Yet the embattled Catholic in Ulster had his back to the wall and was virtually abandoned. There was but a single moment of national outrage—after Bloody Sunday, when the British Embassy was burned down by a Dublin mob. For the most part, the people in the Republic sat on their hands and, moreover, considered Ulster as some place far away and alien.

When hundreds of Belfast Catholics evacuated to the South, they were greeted with anything but open arms. These refugees returned with severe doubts about their own identity.

The Republic is weary from its own millennium of strife. For the first time it is getting a taste of prosperity. If truth be known, it doesn't want the headache and heartache that would come with the annexation of a million hostile Protestants. So, it is left up to the politically impotent IRA to be the keeper of the dream. The Republic's greatest fear is of being sucked into the strife by having to come to the rescue of the Ulster Catholics.

For the first time in the history of the Republic a Prime Minister, Liam Cosgrave, has taken a realistic and honest stance on the matter. He has gone on record as stating that the will of the majority of the people of Ulster must be respected. This is refreshing candor in contrast to the hearts-and-flowers, barroom brand of Republicanism.

The most disillusioned of any party in the Ulster odyssey must be the Protestants. It is apparent they have been used in a venture and are no longer wanted. Their beloved British connection is frayed to the snapping point.

Their dilemma could best be illustrated by an interview with Chichester-Clark, who cited a kind of confusion that is universal. When asked if he was British or Irish, he replied that he was British. He qualified it by saying that he wasn't actually British but of British background. When pressed further as to whether he considered himself at all Irish, Chichester-Clark answered, "I'm an Ulsterman." He admitted that Ulster was part of Ireland, and when finally asked if he was Irish or British, he answered, "I don't know."

Herein lies the heart of the matter. The Ulsterman who lived in the belief he was British now finds out he isn't and that the British don't want him. The Catholic of Ulster has recently discovered he is not wanted in or by the Republic. It is apparent that these unwanted Ulster people ought to get together.

The Protestant case against a United Ireland rests on some shaky timbers. The principal concept of the British connection is all but vanished. The paranoid fear is of Rome, and Paisley's Reformation hogwash expresses just that.

Obviously there are differences, but Catholics and Protestants in the rest of the world live with those differences. Protestant complaints about the Catholic position on divorce, censorship, and birth control are simply no longer valid. The paramount issue is that of an integrated public school system so that bigotry cannot be perpetuated from the incubator. As it is now, "R" for Reformation is branded on the forehead of every Protestant newborn and he's not allowed to live a day without remembering it.

The most telling Protestant argument is that any form of union with Ireland would create an economic hardship. The standard of living and the social benefits are much higher in Ulster. Britain already recognizes that she will have to guarantee parity between North and South until the Irish standard of living has reached the Ulster level. In fact, the Republic has always been tied to Britain economically, and ties will be even closer with their mutual membership in the Common Market. The way that Britain's economy is foundering, it might not take all that long for the Irish to catch up.

The only solution one can realistically envision is the emergence of two equal states, each with great autonomy, within an Irish federation, and a new kind of British connection in the form of an economic union. At the moment it seems like a mad race toward self-destruction. Mistrust and hatred are epic in dimension. Violence is a long established order of life.

The situation continues to deteriorate, with the extremists on both sides winning out. The Paisleyites, with the support of Ulster's Protestants, have gained control, and even William Craig is considered too moderate. Intellectuals and professionals, sensing impending doom, are bailing out, denuding the province of all reason. A place like Ulster in particular cannot afford to lose people like the Reverend Joe Parker and the McCluskeys, who have gone.

The most pressing need of all cannot be legislated—for how does one pass laws compelling a human being to be compassionate and have a sense of justice? The nightmare of Ulster has come about with Christian fighting Christian in one of the most advanced of Western societies. Continuation of this travesty with God can lead to the eclipse of civilization in that part of the world.

PROTESTANT DEFENDER

APPENDIXES

CHRONOLOGY

B.C.

10,000   Ice Age recedes. No sign of human life in Ireland.

6000   Probable date of first human settlement. It is believed a land bridge existed from Scotland and settlers were Scandinavian migrants, mainly foragers.

6000–   Stone Age. Neolithic farmers and tomb builders.
2000

700   Bronze Age metal workings.

350   Celtic migration. With superior iron weapons, they overrun natives.

A.D.

300   High Kingdom established at Tara.

350   Earliest Gaelic writings. Celtic raids on British coast.

400   O'Neill dynasty founded in Ulster.

432   St. Patrick's mission to Ireland establishes Christianity and opens a golden era of religion, literature, education, and missions.

700   Brehon Laws define the ranks of kings, nobles, and commoners, and the rights and status of each—based on a hierarchy and tribal pales. These laws remain until the plantation of Ulster in the early 1600s.

795   Viking raiders hit and run on Irish coast.

800   Ireland's most famous antiquity, the Book of Kells, is illuminated.

800–1000   Viking raids penetrate deeper inland. Cities of Dublin, Cork, and Waterford are founded.

975–1014   Brian Boru becomes High King at Tara.

1014   Vikings defeated at Clontarf, ending their influence. Brian Boru killed during the battle.

1154   Henry II of England obtains a papal bull enabling him to possess Ireland as part of the crown inheritance.

1169–72   Norman invasion sealed by Strongbow coming from Wales. Henry II declared King of Ireland.

1172–   Normans become the "Old English," but integrate into Irish culture and
1250   society completely.

1315–18   Invasion from Scotland by Edward Bruce in league with the O'Neills. After occupation of Ulster and declaration of himself as King of Ireland, Bruce is killed in battle and the invasion defeated.

1366   The Statutes of Kilkenny. For fear that the Normans are becoming too Irish, the Statutes are adopted, forbidding Normans to take on the manners, fashion, and language of the Irish enemies. Intermarriage declared illegal, as is admitting an Irish storyteller into the house. In effect for two centuries. Punishment could mean confiscation of land.

1494   Poynings' Law enacted. In effect until 1782, this legislation forbade the Anglo-Irish Parliament to convene without prior consent of England. Further, the English must approve in advance the Anglo-Irish intended enactments.

1510–50   The Reformation in Europe. Ireland remains Catholic.

1534   Rising by Silken Thomas Fitzgerald.

1537–41   Henry VIII declared King of Ireland by Irish Parliament and appoints himself head of the Church of Ireland.

1553–58	Queen Mary (Bloody Mary) restores Catholicism in England.
1556	Queen Mary establishes the first plantation, confiscating Counties Leix and Offaly.
1560	Elizabeth I restores Protestantism in England.
1565–67	Shane O'Neill Rising. Death of Shane O'Neill.
1569–1603	Desmond Rising and series of risings in Munster.
1591	Trinity College established in Dublin.
1594–1603	Nine Years' War with risings of O'Donnell and O'Neill in Ulster.
1602	Irish defeated by British at Kinsale.
1603	Belfast founded on Chichester grant.
1607	O'Neills leave for the Continent in the "Flight of the Earls."
1609	Ulster planted on former O'Neill lands by Lowland Scots and English.
1612	Derry given to London guilds and merchants to exploit and fortify under the name of the Honourable Irish Society.
1614–18	Derry walled.
1641–53	Peasant Rising in Ulster joined by Owen Roe O'Neill returning from Continent. Oliver Cromwell campaign results in massacres and confiscation of two and a half million acres of land. Irish are forced west of the river Shannon to "Hell or Connaught."
1685–88	James II, a Catholic, ascends British throne. He is dispossessed, flees England after William of Orange takes over.
1689–91	Jacobite war between James II and William of Orange on Irish soil. Siege of Derry by James unsuccessful. William is victorious at the Battle of the Boyne. Treaty of Limerick ends war.
1695	"Flight of the Wild Geese" as bulk of Irish Army goes to the Continent.
1695–1725	Penal Laws enacted to crush Catholics and Catholicism. Restrictions on Irish trade. Irish woolen industry crippled by England.
1700–1800	Presbyterians in Ulster come under some of the Penal Laws and begin a mass Scotch-Irish exodus to America.
1710–95	Ribbonmen, Peep-o'-Day Boys, Volunteers, and other secret organizations form up and night-ride in vicious peasant land wars.
1782–1800	Penal Laws relaxed. Grattan's Parliament in Dublin compels Westminster to abrogate its authority to legislate for Ireland and gains Irish autonomy.
1791	Theobald Wolfe Tone forms United Irishmen in Belfast.
1795	Battle of the Diamond fought outside Armagh by Catholic Volunteers and the victorious Protestant Peep-o'-Day Boys. The Orange Order is formed to celebrate.
1798	United Irish Rising crushed. Death of Wolfe Tone.
1800	Act of Union under British Prime Minister Pitt forces Irish Parliament to dissolve and Ireland to become part of the United Kingdom.
1803	Unsuccessful rising by Robert Emmet. Emmet immortalizes himself in his speech from the dock before his execution.
1823–43	The era of Daniel O'Connell in which emancipation is won for the Catholics.
1845	Queens College founded in Belfast.
1845–48	Young Ireland movement founded. Young Ireland Rising fails.
1845–50	Crop failure, British landlordism, and governmental incompetence result in famine. A million Irish peasants die by hunger and disease and another million flee, mainly to America.

1850	Tenant League founded.
1858–67	The era of the Fenians, a secret organization with heavy Irish-American backing. The Fenian Rising fails.
1869–70	Under British Prime Minister Gladstone, legislation is enacted to disestablish the Anglican Church as the Church of Ireland. Land reforms enacted.
1877–91	The era of Charles Stewart Parnell as "uncrowned King of Ireland." Parnell becomes a major political force by attaining leadership of the Irish Party in Westminster, leading the fight for the abolition of the Act of Union to be replaced by Irish Home Rule. Parnell is destroyed in a divorce scandal and succumbs without reaching his goals.
1884	Founding of the Gaelic Athletic Association, which not only revives the old games but proves a boon to nationalism.
1885	Unionist Party formed to fight Gladstone's Home Rule Act. The Orange card played by Randolph Churchill.
1893	The Gaelic League formed as forerunner of the cultural revival which becomes extremely nationalistic in character.
1899–1904	Arthur Griffith founds the Republican paper, *The United Irishman,* and later, Sinn Fein political party.
1912–14	The Third Home Rule Bill passes. Protestant Ulster holds Covenant Day, declaring an Act of Covenant of loyalty to Britain. Protestants arm and run guns into province. Home Rule Bill suspended by beginning of World War I.
1916	Republican Rising during Easter Week. Leaders executed.
1917–21	Sinn Fein wins election. Republic declared. De Valera named President. Lloyd George rejects Irish claim and Anglo-Irish War ensues with Black and Tan terror.
1920	Act of Ireland offers dual dominion status to Ireland and Ulster, abrogating the Third Home Rule Act.
1921	Ulster Parliament opens. Irish delegation goes to London and a truce is declared. The Irish Dail rejects the terms and after further negotiations a Treaty is signed by Michael Collins after an ultimatum by Lloyd George. De Valera repudiates Treaty.
1922	Dail approves the Treaty by a narrow margin. De Valera resigns, the nation splits. After an Irish attempt to solve the situation, Lloyd George pressures Pro-Treaty forces to denounce the Anti-Treaty forces and an Irish Civil War ensues. The Irish Free State is established in twenty-six counties.
1922	In Ulster B-Specials are formed and Special Powers enacted.
1923–25	Civil War ends with thousands of Anti-Treaty men and women interned. Ulster ends proportional representation, begins gerrymandering, and refuses to change borders.
1926	De Valera founds Fianna Fail Party.
1932	De Valera comes to power, relaxes statutes on the IRA. Land annuities to Britain canceled and Treaty renounced. All of Ireland claimed, and oath to the Crown is abolished. This leads to a trade and economic war with England.
1934	The Blueshirts, a quasi-fascist movement, makes a brief and unsuccessful appearance.
1937	New constitution declares Irish sovereignty.
1938–45	Ill-fated IRA bomb campaign against British cities prelude to World War II. In a move to keep Ireland neutral de Valera invokes internment on the IRA.
1949	The Republic of Ireland is declared, damaging claims to the six counties of Ulster.

1956–57	IRA campaigns against the Ulster border are badly conceived and end in failure.
1964	Riots at Divis Flats in Belfast. Terence O'Neill elected Prime Minister of Northern Ireland. Civil Rights movement founded in Dungannon.
1966	Paisley agitation against Civil Righters heightens. O'Neill invokes Special Powers Act after Malvern Street murder of Catholics by outlawed Ulster Volunteer Force.
1968	Civil Rights movement snowballs. Royal Ulster Constabulary baton charge at Derry gains world attention.
1969	Paisley mob attacks Civil Rights march at Burntollet Bridge. B-Specials mobilized. Orange and Apprentice Boys parades incite riots. Constabulary and B-Specials beaten in the Battle of Bogside. Riots in Belfast. Catholics burned out in Ardoyne. O'Neill resigns.
1971	First British soldiers killed by execution. Chichester-Clark resigns. Internment invoked.
1972	Bloody Sunday in Derry. Stormont government falls to direct rule from London. William Whitelaw named Supremo by Heath. Ulster reels under bomb campaign by IRA. Sectarian murders begun by Protestants in revenge. Bloody Friday in Belfast as IRA sets off two dozen bombs in less than two hours. Twenty thousand British troops in Ulster. Operation Motorman breaks barricades as British troops enter Free Derry.
1973	Proposals for new governmental alignment accepted by middle-of-the-road parties on both sides. Catholic and Protestant extremists vow to destroy the plan. De Valera retires as President of the Republic. Lynch government falls to Fianna Gael-Labour Coalition. Erskine Childers, a Protestant and son of a Republican martyr, elected President of the Republic. Council of Ireland, with extremely limited powers, agreed upon by North and South. Catholic/Protestant power-sharing coalition initiated November 21 in Ulster with Brian Faulkner as leader. Militant wing of Unionist Party rejects coalition and bolts, leaving government badly weakened.
1974	Militant Protestants sweep election. Bernadette Devlin ousted. Labor Party returns to power in England. Harold Wilson again Prime Minister. Dublin bombed without warning. Militants from Ulster suspected. General strike by Ulster Protestants brings down coalition. Direct rule re-invoked by Harold Wilson. Swedish Academy names Sean MacBride Nobel Peace Laureate.
1975	New Supremo, Merlyn Rees, fails to stabilize Ulster. IRA intensifies bomb campaigns in England in effort to have British public opinion force government to remove troops from Ulster. De Valera dies.
1976	Ulster situation continues to deteriorate, with failure of all attempts at reconciliation, power sharing, or coalition. Province edges closer to civil war.
1977	Betty Williams and Mairead Corrigan awarded Nobel prize for their effort to end bloodshed in Northern Ireland.

JILLY

When I strapped a Mickey Mouse watch on her wrist, she broke into a wide grin. Then I gave her the first copy of my novel, *QB VII*, which had been dedicated to her on her twenty-third birthday. She opened it and acted as though she were reading the inscription. When she closed it she saw my picture on the back and she held it against her cheek, then impulsively sat up, threw her arms open, and said, "So much love!"

Jill could neither tell time nor read. The black circles beneath her eyes, the gauntness of body, and her head heavily swathed in bandages told a chilling story. She had just emerged from a coma of several days after brain surgery, the result of an accident on Long Island.

I talked with the doctor, then drove back to the motel. My partner, Walt Smith, and I were working day and night to get our musical *Ari* ready for Broadway. After the accident we took rooms near Port Jefferson so we could be close at hand.

"We've got to prepare ourselves, Walt," I told him. "We're not going to get the same Jill back."

She was born Jill Peabody in 1947, a Bostonian down the line. Long before teen age, she had given up dolls for a camera.

Formal photographic training came at Harvard, Colorado College, and New York University. She went through a series of the unglamorous kinds of work one does out there with the ducks to earn one's spurs. The turning point came through the Center of the Eye, a photographic institute then in Aspen where she studied, taught children, and later joined the staff as associate director.

Leon Uris

Alex Gotfryd

I met Jill after my own life had bottomed out with the death of my wife. She gave me the world again. We were married in February 1970 at the Algonquin Hotel. By then, she was an artist with the camera and a highly accomplished technician, a thorough professional.

Doctors still shake their heads in disbelief over her "miraculous" recovery, extremely rare in such a case. Certainly God's will was in league with the skill of a great surgeon. But there was more. During her fight for life, and to regain her health, she embodied all that is splendid in the human spirit, and her victory was beyond mere inspirational.

Within eighteen months this girl was leaping, camera in hand, out of helicopters, working under gunfire and behind dangerous barricades, scaling cliffs, crouched behind the goal line in wild Irish games, elbowing through mobs, edging to the brink of high buildings exposed to sniper sights.

I think that Jill's real accomplishment was to be able to turn on to every sort of photographic demand. She had to cover the full range from high fashion to portrait work to tough street journalism to children to sports to nature work and getting to the innards of the human soul. She was good to start with, and she grew every day.

With it all, no part of being a wife and partner suffered because of her staggering work load. The home was always beautiful, the meals magnificent, the accounts up to date, and a husband very happy. Of the latter, she says, "I'm not the writer, I'm the nurse." All this was accomplished with a calm disposition and a total absence of hysteria.

I suppose that what personifies her most is that Saturday morning she photographed the Moore Street Market. We were giving a formal dinner that night, and as she moved about taking photographs she stopped at numerous stalls and made purchases . . . moving about, camera in the right hand, shopping bag in the left.

When asked how she managed it all, she expounded a bit of her philosophy. "Photography is my minor, the writer is my major." Now this concept may seem rather old-fashioned in light of today's libertarians. On the other hand, there's nothing unequal about it at all . . . when two people feel exactly the same way.

PHOTOGRAPHING IRELAND

by Jill Uris

My first sight of Ireland came in the autumn of 1971 in five days of travel from Cork to Shannon. It was enough time to get a whiff of the magic of the country I would come to love. It was the existence of life in a Godforsaken landscape, the sorcery of a rainbow over a castle or, perhaps, the lady I picked up on the road who blessed me with words of Joyce and insisted I join her for tea in her home. The blending of expressive faces with awesome scenery told me I was in a photographer's heaven.

Lee and I returned to embark on two projects, this book and his novel. Lesson number one in photographing Ireland is to appreciate the weather. There are unseen benefits of rain and the ever changing light of those "soft Irish mists." Using rain as an ally can give a delicate quality to photographs impossible to capture in bright sunlight.

Two days after our arrival, on Easter Sunday, we came upon an IRA commemoration in the cemetery of a small Connemara town. The mood was mellow and sad and the faces warm and resigned. It was pouring and the muted quality of the photographs expressed the pensiveness of the moment perfectly.

On the following day, Easter Monday, we traveled to Carrickfergus in Ulster, where a Protestant rally took place. It was as bright and sunny as the previous day had been wet. Orangemen's faces matched their harsh slogans, and the severe light emphasized the starkness of the occasion.

We went into Ireland with open minds and open hearts and were rewarded with continual discovery. Traveling and working as a team, we quickly learned the luxury of each other's vision and thoughts. From our constant dialogue a second marriage developed, this one between pictures and story.

The richest part of the country, both spiritually and photographically, is the West. In addition to the dramatic scenery there is a refreshing absence of automobiles and modern shopping centers. The people are an integral part of the landscape. For the most part I found them natural and not self-conscious. Perhaps that stems from a philosophy that demands little from life and that measures wealth by use of language and warmth of spirit. Although they are not a physically beautiful people, I found it easy to make beautiful pictures of them.

Photographing in the Republic was almost always a joy. Ulster was another story. For starters, being a woman posed certain difficulties, and Lee wasn't always there to run interference for me, be it shoving through crowds to get up on platforms or getting moved around by bully boys who refused to take me seriously. Otherwise, being a woman, you are apt to stand out, and we found that returning to sensitive areas aroused suspicions and became downright dangerous.

Urban guerrilla warfare produces a paranoid society. No one knows who the enemy is, where the enemy is, or when the enemy will strike. Everyone is suspicious and especially suspicious of a camera. On one occasion I nearly had my film confiscated after photographing what appeared to be a public parade, but it happened that I was pointing at an IRA leader who was on the run. The general rule was to ask permission if trouble could be avoided that way. Otherwise we would have to run the risk in order to get the picture.

The streets were the hairiest. There was no permission to be granted and I had to move fast and inconspicuously. Protestant neighborhoods were very touchy, so we used various techniques and decoys to camouflage the camera. We had a skillful driver who could U-turn on a halfpenny at the right instant for me to shoot and I became adept at working with three cameras from all parts of the car. If time was needed we would buy it by inventing trouble under the hood or by some other ploy to take attention away from me. The technical quality of some of the street photographs suffered because of the speed with which I had to work and the interference of windows.

Gun battles and explosions are the most dramatic elements of street war but the most difficult to photograph. The real impact is essentially one of sound, of gunfire, and unfortunately a soldier in the midst of a gunfight might look as posed as a TV cowboy. Bomb explosions are certainly visual if one catches the exact instant the debris is flying. The closest we got to a real blockbuster was a bomb placed next to our hotel. I was glad it was neutralized and I didn't get the picture.

Although we had access to close-in fighting, neither Lee nor I cared to photograph people bloodied or dead. We did seek out victims in their battered and barricaded neighborhoods. Interviewing and photographing survivors was a most painful experience. We would be completely drained, with just enough energy left to cry. And cry we did. I asked myself over and over, "How can children be made to hate each other this way? How can Christians hate each other this way?" After having

would have created undue risk, Lee carried a small Rollei B35 and was able to get some otherwise impossible photographs.

All the photographs were shot by me except for the dozen that Lee took and the one picture of Maud Gonne in which I photographed a photograph. Everything was taken with available light and without color-correction filters.

My equipment included a Nikon and Nikkormat with four lenses ranging from 28mm. to 200mm. I found this particularly good for journalistic and other fast work.

The Rollei B35, because of its size, was extremely useful for sensitive situations.

A Hasselblad with 50-mm., 80-mm., and 20-mm. lenses was used for scenics and portraits. My film was Tri-X, Ektachrome X, and Ektachrome High Speed, and a few rolls of Plus X and Kodak CPS.

looked into their faces, the faces of people who have the ugliest kind of war on their own front steps, I feel a little less naïve and a little more understanding, for I know that I too, would fight back.

We were fortunate to have Geraldine Kelly as our associate. She did it all, from the never ending battle of getting appointments to being the "fixer" to lending herself as an abstract model. She was many things to us and, not the least, our teacher of things Irish.

James Pozarik and Jay Wyman assisted me greatly in the darkroom detail and Connie Mannlein was a bulwark on research.

My trusty assistant, Leon Uris, aside from being porter of the camera bags, chauffeur, and hatchetman when need be, acquitted himself beautifully when given a camera. On occasions when we had to be in different places or when my presence

ACKNOWLEDGMENTS

Obviously, we required special co-operation from dozens of varied sources. We were blessed. Those who opted out on our requests could be counted on one hand. Perhaps the opinions expressed in many cases were not what certain individuals and groups had hoped for, but we made no deals in exchange for assistance. We listened carefully to everyone's point of view, then tried to present the truth as we saw it.

A great number of those who participated with us might now be embarrassed by an acknowledgment. For others, mention of their names could endanger their lives. We had earlier concluded that this should be an "all or nothing" sort of acknowledgment. Those who helped us know they did and we are grateful. We pray that something we have done here may shed some understanding and do its own small thing toward peace.

GERALDINE KELLY *of Dungarvan and Dublin. Special assistant, project co-ordinator, and dear friend.*

BOB MOON *of the Shankill, Belfast. He lived dangerously, serving all journalists, including ourselves, as a war zone driver. He died too young, of a heart attack. When asked his religion on a government form, he replied, "Taxi Driver." May his soul find the peace that eluded him in life.*